D1130357

WITHDRAWN
No longer the property of the
Boston Public Library.
Sale of this material benefits the Library

Continental Glass

*Published titles in the Collectors' Handbook
series edited by Robert Keith Middlemas*

ENGLISH AND IRISH ANTIQUE GLASS
Derek Davis

BRITISH POTTERY AND PORCELAIN
Geoffrey Godden

CLOCKS AND WATCHES 1400–1900
Eric Bruton

FURNITURE IN ENGLAND:
THE AGE OF THE JOINER
S. W. Wolsey and R. W. P. Luff

ISLAMIC RUGS
Kudret H. Turkhan

FRENCH SILVER
Frank Davis

Continental Glass

FRANK DAVIS

Praeger Publishers

New York · Washington

BOOKS THAT MATTER

Published in the United States of America
in 1972 by Praeger Publishers, Inc.
111 Fourth Avenue, New York,
N.Y. 10003

© 1972, in London, England, by Frank Davis

All rights reserved

Library of Congress Catalog Card Number: 79 – 180728

✱ NK 5/42
.D3
1972

BOSTON PUBLIC LIBRARY
3.74

Printed in Great Britain

Contents

		Page
	List of Illustrations	vi
	Preface and Acknowledgements	xv
1	Introduction	1
2	The Twilight of Rome	8
3	Spain	23
4	The Netherlands	36
5	France	50
6	Bohemia, Germany and Austria	73
7	The Nineteenth Century and After	87
	Epilogue	115
	Appendix: Rock-Crystal	117
	Selected Bibliography	119
	Index	121

List of Illustrations

1 The Portland Vase. Cut cameo fashion, opaque white on blue, height 9⅝ ins, late 1st century BC or 1st century AD. *British Museum*.

2 The Lycurgus Cup. Opaque green but wine-coloured when viewed by transmitted light, height 6½ ins, 4th century AD. *British Museum*.

3 Roman glass plaque, cobalt blue, height 7⅙ ins, 1st century AD. *British Museum*.

4 Flask of greenish glass, height 6⅛ ins, late 2nd century AD, from Cyprus. *British Museum*.

5 Handled flagon, bluish-green, rim out-splayed and folded up and in, height 11¼ ins, third quarter 1st century AD, found at Barnwell, Cambridgeshire. *British Museum*.

6 Wine-coloured jar with opaque white masks and white stripes on the handles, rim folded down, up and in, concave neck, height 9¾ ins, 1st century AD, found in Campania, Italy. *British Museum*.

7 Bowl, greenish glass with dark blue blobs, diameter 7⅝ ins, 4th century AD, from Cyprus. *British Museum*.

8 Bluish-green bottle, rim folded outwards, upwards and inwards, height 7⅞ ins, 1st or 2nd century AD, found at Faversham, Kent. *British Museum*.

9 Ribbed bowl, bluish-green, rim folded out and down, diameter 7½ ins, 3rd century AD, found at Faversham, Kent. *British Museum*.

10 Slender flagon, olive green, rim outsplayed and folded up and in, height 9⅛ ins, late 1st or early 2nd century AD, from Bayford, Kent. *British Museum*.

11 Bluish-green flagon, four pinches on rim to strengthen handle, height 7⅞ ins, late 2nd or early 3rd century AD, from Bayford, Kent. *British Museum*.

12 Greenish-colourless jug, height 9⅞ ins, 4th century AD, from Andernach, Germany. *British Museum*.

13 Buff colourless bowl, facet-cut, diameter 5⅝ ins, 2nd century AD, from a grave at Leuna-Merseburg, Germany. *British Museum*.

14 Claw beaker, green glass, height 7½ ins, *c.* 600 AD, found at Castle Eden, Co. Durham. *British Museum*.

15 Standing cup and cover, colourless glass, gilt ribs, above them blue and white thread, red dots, etc., height 16⅝ ins, second half 15th century. *British Museum.*

16 Goblet and cover, clear colourless glass with enamelled and gilt decoration, height 18 ins, late 15th century. *Victoria and Albert Museum.*

17 Enamelled bowl, height 6½ ins, 15th century. *British Museum.*

18 Standing cup, sapphire blue, height 6½ ins, mid 15th century. *British Museum.*

19 Emerald green goblet, ornamented with portrait medallions, young man and auburn haired girl supported by cupid, height 8⅝ ins, second half 15th century. *British Museum.*

20 Plate, opaque glass painted in red San Giorgio Maggiore, height 8⅞ ins, 1741. *British Museum.*

21 Two-handled vase, opaque white, 17th century. *Victoria and Albert Museum.*

22 Covered beaker, opaque white, painted with rural scene, early 18th century. *Victoria and Albert Museum.*

23 Bottle, opaque white, coat of arms on neck enamelled, inscription on base 'Murano Miotti', height 9⅜ ins, 1747. *British Museum.*

24 Tazza, colourless glass, diamond-point engraving, chain motif in centre in blue, diameter 10⅝ ins, early 17th century, perhaps Spanish. *British Museum.*

25 Goblet, colourless glass, latticino, late 16th century, perhaps S. Netherlands. *British Museum.*

26 Three glasses: *left* goblet, blue, white, red and gold, height 7¼ ins, late 15th century; *centre* goblet, white, blue and gold, height 6½ ins, early 16th century; *right* covered cup, diamond-point engraving, early 16th century. *Christie's.*

27 Gadrooned bowl with blue threads, hollow spreading foot, dark blue border, height 10⅞ ins, mid 15th century. *Sotheby's.*

28 Nef (ship), clear, turquoise and green glass, height 15 ins, 16th century. *Sotheby's.*

29 Goblet, colourless glass with three masqueraders, height 7½ ins, late 16th century. *British Museum.*

30 *Left* tazza, latticino spiral motif radiating from a central boss, diameter 10½ ins, c.1600; *centre* bowl, enamelled in pale blue, white and gold with floral ornaments, ribbed moulded base, diameter 7¼ ins, 16th century; *right* tazza, blue and red dots, diameter 9⅜ ins, 16th century. *Sotheby's.*

31 Bottle, moulded with band of two lions and two double-headed eagles, swirling bands of latticino, height 7¼ ins, 17th century. *Sotheby's.*

32 Vase, enamelled in the Venetian manner, transparent uncoloured glass, height 10¾ ins, 16th century, Barcelona. *Victoria and Albert Museum.*

33   Vase, transparent green glass, threading and pincered decoration with eight tubular handles, height 7¾ ins, 16th century, probably Almeria Province. *Victoria and Albert Museum.*

34   Vase, transparent smoky yellow glass, threading and pincered decoration, height 7 ins, 17th century, Granada Province. *Victoria and Albert Museum.*

35   Double cruet, green glass with internal partition, trailed threading and pincered cresting on single handle, height 6⅝ ins, 18th century, probably Granada Province. *Victoria and Albert Museum.*

36   Vase, transparent green glass with threading and pincered decoration, height 6¾ ins, 18th century, Granada Province. *Victoria and Albert Museum.*

37   Botijo, transparent yellow green glass with threading, trailed chain and pincered decoration, height 8¼ ins, 17th century, Granada Province. *Victoria and Albert Museum.*

38   *Left* vase, Venetian style, yellowish glass, opaque-white combed decoration, height 6⅛ ins, 16th or 17th century, Barcelona; *centre* small jug, façon de Venise, opaque-white strands, blue handle, height 5⅛ ins, early 17th century, probably Barcelona; *right* biberon, opaque-white tape and twisted latticino, façon de Venise, 17th or 18th century, perhaps Spanish. *Sotheby's.*

39   Vase, transparent blue-green glass, overlaid with dark brown, brown handles and threading, height 5⅝ ins, 17th or 18th century, Granada Province. *Victoria and Albert Museum.*

40   Oil lamp, transparent blue-green glass, height 5⅛ ins, 17th or 18th century, Granada Province. *Victoria and Albert Museum.*

41   Jug, pale straw-coloured glass, frosted, tooled handle, height 7½ ins, late 16th or early 17th century, Catalonia. *Victoria and Albert Museum.*

42   *Left* vase, green glass streaked with brown diagonal ribbing, height 8 1/16 ins, 18th century, probably Recuenco; *right* vase, uncoloured glass with diagonal ribbing, height 7⅞ ins, 18th century, probably Recuenco. *Victoria and Albert Museum.*

43   Covered jar, crystal glass, engraved and fire gilt, faceted knob, height 20 ins, 1775–85, La Granja de San Ildefonso. *Victoria and Albert Museum.*

44   Tray, crystal glass blown in the mould, engraved and fire gilt, 6¼ ins wide,· 1775–85, La Granja de San Ildefonso. *Victoria and Albert Museum.*

45   Decanter, crystal glass blown in a fluted mould and enamelled, height 12½ ins, 1775–85, La Granja de San Ildefonso. *Victoria and Albert Museum.*

46   Cruet (canadella), transparent straw-tinted glass, opaque-white combing, finial, vermicular collar, lip and foot plain, height 6 ins, late 16th century, Catalonia. *Pilkington Museum.*

47   Wine jug, blue-green glass, swan neck strap handle, the body decorated with ribs, spiral trail around the four lips, mid 18th century. *Pilkington Museum.*

48   Vase, two-handled, 16th or 17th century, Andalusia or possibly Castile. *Victoria and Albert Museum.*

49   Jug, opaque white with bands of clear glass in between, silver-gilt mount London 1548–9, height 6¼ ins, first half 16th century. *British Museum.*

50   Tazza, colourless glass, gilt prunts, height 6¼ ins, second half 16th century, S. Netherlands probably Antwerp. *British Museum.*

51   'Ice' glass, three lion masks, height 7⅞ ins, second half 16th century, S. Netherlands, probably Antwerp. *British Museum.*

52   Goblet, façon de Venise, white spiral decoration, height 11 ins, 17th century. *Christie's.*

53   Beaker, swirling opaque-white threads, façon de Venise, height 5¼ ins. *Walter F. Smith Collection, Sotheby's.*

54   Wine glass, façon de Venise, diamond-point inscription, funnel bowl, height 6½ ins, 17th century. *Sotheby's.*

55   *Left* glass, diamond engraved, façon de Venise, yellow orange and white convoluted stem, pincered blue wings, height 7⅝ ins, second half 17th century, perhaps Netherlands; *centre* façon de Venise, diamond engraved, winged and pincered stem with blue scrolls, height 6¼ ins, 17th century; *right* façon de Venise, knopped and pincered serpent stem, ornamented in blue, height 7⅝ ins, 17th century, perhaps Liège. *Sotheby's.*

56   Drinking horn, diamond-point engraving '1595 21 Julet', colourless glass, length 12⅜ ins, late 16th century, probably S. Netherlands. *British Museum.*

57   Goblet, emerald green, gilt heraldic decoration, height 6⅝ ins, *c.*1600. *British Museum.*

58   Roemer, greenish glass, height 6⅛ ins, second half 17th century. *Pilkington Brothers.*

59   Stangenglas, amber-green tint, height 8⅛ ins, 16th century, S. Netherlands. *British Museum.*

60   Barrel-shaped glass, green glass with six finger grips, height 7⅞ ins, 17th century, Germany or Netherlands. *British Museum.*

61   Roemer, greenish glass, diamond engraving, inscription in Dutch 'Still lives Orange', height 5¼ ins, second quarter 17th century. *British Museum.*

62   Roemer, diamond engraved, attributed to Anna Visscher, height 5¾ ins, *c.*1650, *Victoria and Albert Museum.*

63   Glass, diamond engraved by William Mooleyser, height 8 ins, *c.*1685. *Victoria and Albert Museum.*

64   Roemer, diamond engraved by G.V.Nes, Arms of William and of the seven united Provinces, height 9⅝ ins, *c.*1687. *Victoria and Albert Museum.*

65   Stangenglas, greenish glass, raspberry prunts, height 11¾ ins, late 16th or early 17th century, S. Netherlands or Rhineland. *British Museum.*

66 Still life by Pieter Claes showing a beaker with prunts, signed and dated 1627. *Parke-Bernet.*

67 Still life by Jacob van Es showing two types of glasses, 17th century. *Sotheby's.*

68 Goblet, faintly yellowish glass engraved with diamond-point, inscription, height 7¾ ins. c.1660. *Victoria and Albert Museum.*

69 Bottle, engraved by Willem van Heemskerk, height 10⅜ ins, 1674. *Victoria and Albert Museum.*

70 Goblet and cover, diamond engraved, height 10 ins, c.1670. *Christie.*

71 Flute, colourless glass, diamond-point half length portrait of a young boy, coat of arms of House of Orange, inscribed 'Wilhelmus Prince d'Orange', height 15¾ ins, c.1660. *British Museum.*

72 Goblet, probably decorated 1657–8, Mary, Princess Royal of England eldest daughter of Charles I and Henrietta of England, height 6⅜ ins. *British Museum.*

73 Goblet, stipple engraved by Wolff, The Hague, height 7¼ ins, 1791, probably Newcastle. *British Museum.*

74 English glass, stipple engraved by Wolff in Holland, height 7¼ ins. 1775–90. *Victoria and Albert Museum.*

75 Armorial glass, stipple engraved by David Wolff, arms of William V of Orange, Newcastle glass, knopped stem, conical foot, height 6⅞ ins *Sotheby's.*

76 Covered goblet, English glass of lead, engraved in Holland by Jacob Sang 1757, inscription, height 19½ ins. *British Museum.*

77 Beaker with three halberdiers. *Musée de Cluny.*

78 Goblet with the portrait of Pierre Tallon. *Musée de Cluny.*

79 Goblet with the arms of Louis XII and Anne de Bretagne. *Musée de Cluny.*

80 Pommeraye goblet. *Musée de Cluny.*

81 Enamelled goblet, height 6⅜ ins, mid 16th century. *British Museum.*

82 Colourless glass, height 8⅝ ins, 16th century. *Musée des Arts Decoratifs.*

83 Vase, two-handled, colourless, height 14⅝ ins, early 17th century. *Musée des Arts Decoratifs.*

84 Goblet on bell foot, façon de Venise, height 7¼ ins, 17th century. *Musée des Arts Decoratifs.*

85 Beaker, octagonal sided, height 3 ins, 17th century. *Musée des Arts Decoratifs.*

86 The Amiens Chalice. Height 6¼ ins, late 17th century. *British Museum.*

87 Moulded beaker from Orleans, by Bernard Perrot, mark – three fleurs de lys and a unicorn, the figures possibly intended for Louis XIV and Madame de Maintenon, height 3 ins, late 17th century. *Sotheby's.*

88 Moulded pot, colourless glass, diameter 3½ ins, 18th century. *Musée des Arts Decoratifs.*

89 Three glasses from the Midi, 18th century: *left* Silesian stem; *centre* drawn trumpet bowl with tear; *right* drawn trumpet bowl; all three apparently façon d'Anglais. *Musée des Arts Decoratifs.*

90 Three glasses, façon de Venise, height 5⅞ ins, 18th century. *Musée des Arts Decoratifs.*

91 Covered goblet, burette and jug, height 8⅝ ins, 18th century. *Musée des Arts Decoratifs.*

92 Lamp, clear glass, height 10⅝ ins, 18th century. *Musée des Arts Decoratifs.*

93 Goblet, façon de Venise, late 16th or early 17th century, perhaps French. *Victoria and Albert Museum.*

94 Sweetmeat vase and cover (*Drageoir*), mourning girl beside a broken column monument inscribed 'Cigit L'Indifferent', height 6¼ ins, 18th century, Eastern France. *Musée des Arts Decoratifs.*

95 Marbled glass pilgrim bottle, 18th century. *Victoria and Albert Museum.*

96 Equestrian statue of Henri IV by Charles-François Hazard (1758–1812), 18th century, Nevers. *Musée des Arts Decoratifs.*

97 The Judgement of Paris, height 8¼ ins, 1777, Nevers. *Musée des Arts Decoratifs.*

98 The Basket of Glasses, painting by Sebastien Stoskopf. *Musées de la ville de Strasbourg.*

99 Glass plaque engraved by Caspar Lehman, 1619 and 1620. *Victoria and Albert Museum.*

100 Covered goblet, height 11 ins, c.1700, Silesian. *Sotheby's.*

101 Covered goblet, engraved with 'SCR' beneath crown, deep blue, height 12¼ ins, 1701–5, Potsdam. *British Museum.*

102 Still life by Floris van Schooten, 17th century. *Brod Gallery.*

103 Three glasses, one 17th century Roemer, two Stangengläser, German. *Sotheby's.*

104 Beaker, ruby glass, height 4 ins, end of 17th century. *Sotheby's.*

105 Square flask, enamelled with St Christopher carrying the Child Jesus, 1697, Bohemia. *Sotheby's.*

106 Armorial Humpen, enamelled in colours, 1683, Saxony. *Sotheby's.*

107 Two goblets, c.1740; covered beaker, c.1791. *Sotheby's.*

108 Jug, enamelled, dated 1573, Bohemian. *Sotheby's.*

109 Secular glass, enamelled hunt scene, clear glass tinted grey, height 26.2 cm, late 16th century, Bohemia. *British Museum.*

110 Ecclesiastical goblet, Zwischengoldglas, height 7⅛ ins; wine glass, Zwischengoldglas, height 5½ ins. *Sotheby's.*

111 Goblet, height 11¼ ins, Bohemian. *Museum of Applied Arts, Prague.*

112 Decanter jug, Ravenscroft, wheel-engraved with The Toilet of Venus in German or Low Countries workshop, c.1676. *Sotheby's.*

113 Beaker, dark blue enamelled in white, height 6¾ ins, 1599, Bohemia or S. Netherlands. *British Museum.*

114   Covered goblet, Zwischengoldglas, height 10½ ins, *c*.1730, Bohemia. *Sotheby's.*

115   Two Stangengläser, Jacob Praun and his wife Clara, height 11¼ ins and 11 ins, probably 1589, German (or Venice). *British Museum.*

116   Beaker, blue, mauve and green enamels, height 3⅝ ins, late 18th century, Bohemia. *Sotheby's.*

117   Goblet, colourless glass, horsemen in grisaille, touches of lilac, blue and green, background bluish, height 8⅝ ins, *c*.1740, Bohemia. *British Museum.*

118   Ewer and basin, Schwarzlot, decoration chinoiserie attributed to Ignatz Preissler, second quarter of 18th century, Silesia or Bohemia. *British Museum.*

119   Beaker or ice-pail, opaque white, height 9 ins, *c*.1750–70, Bohemia. *British Museum.*

120   Goblet Hall-in-Tyrol, height 7⅜ ins, *c*.1550. *Walter F.Smith collection, Sotheby's.*

121   Covered goblet Hall-in-Tyrol, dark tinted glass, amethyst colour finial, height 15¼ ins, second half 16th century. *Walter F.Smith collection, Sotheby's.*

122   Purple-glass, diamond-point engraving, 9½ ins diameter, 1613. *Sotheby's.*

123   Covered goblet, green glass Nuremburg, engraved by Hermann Schwinger, height 14¼ ins, late 17th century. *Sotheby's.*

124   Passglas, painted in bright enamel colours, height 10⅛ ins, 1719, German. *Sotheby's.*

125   Joke glass, height 11 ins, 17th century, German. *Sotheby's.*

126   Covered goblet, colourless glass, applied gilding in relief, height 14 ins, after 1733–4, Dresden. *British Museum.*

127   Wine glass, enamelled in relief by Johann Fredrick Meyer, height 5½ ins, *c*.1725, Saxon. *Walter F.Smith collection, Sotheby's.*

128   *Left* Humpen, enamelled with the Ages of Man, height 7 ins, 1696, Saxony; *right* Passglas, enamelled with a playing card, height 7¾ ins, Saxony. *Christie's.*

129   Three engraved portraits by Dominik Bimann, 1830s. *Sotheby's.*

130   Tumbler painted by G.S.Mohn, inscribed 'La Reconnaissance', 1812. *Victoria and Albert Museum.*

131   Biedermeier cigar holder, manner of C. von Scheidt, height 6¼ ins. *Sotheby's.*

132   Beaker, Lithyalin, height 4½ ins, *c*.1830. *Victoria and Albert Museum.*

133   Hyalith and Zwischengold Medaillonpokal, height 7⅛ ins. *Sotheby's.*

134   Service designed by Ludwig Lobmeyr, 1856. *J.& L.Lobmeyr.*

135   Service designed by Joseph Hoffman, 1920. *J.& L.Lobmeyr.*

136   Beaker, enamelled on golden wooden base, designed by Lotte Fink, 1925. *J.& L.Lobmeyr.*

137   Crystal vase, designed by Lehmden. *J.& L.Lobmeyr.*

138   Presentation urn, from the Federal President of Austria to the Shah of Persia, height 14 ins, 1966. *J.& L.Lobmeyr.*

139   Crystal plate, cut by Franz Fritsche for Lobmeyr, diameter 8¾ ins, 1870–85. *Municipal Museum Kamenicky Senov.*

140   Engraved jardinière, designer Ludvika Smrckova, form dates from 1935, engraved 1945, height 2⅞ ins. *Property of the designer.*

141   Sorbet glass, belonged to the Empress Josephine, inscribed with letter J and crown, height 3⅜ ins. *Musée des Arts Decoratifs.*

142   Tazza, wheel engraved, height 6¼ ins, 1862, Clichy-La-Garenne. *British Museum.*

143   Flower weight, unrecorded design, 3⅛ ins, Baccarat. *Sotheby's.*

144   *Left* weight, lime yellow ground, 3 ins, St Louis; *centre* weight, faceted green with snake, 2⅞ ins, St Louis; *right* weight, turquoise double overlay, millefiori mushroom, 3³⁄₁₆ ins. *Sotheby's.*

145   The Oak Vase. Height 10 ins, 1895, by Emile Galle at Nancy. *Victoria and Albert Museum.*

146   A liqueur set, clear blue glass with gold and enamelled, height 9¾ ins, Emile Galle. *Sotheby's.*

147   Vase, sweet peas, blue green and white, height 19¾ ins, Daum, influenced by Galle. *Christie's.*

148   Gourd shaped vase, 'graal' glass, 1948, Edward Hald, Orrefors. *Orrefors Glasbruk.*

149   Vase, engraved by Vicke Lindstrand, height 8¼ ins, about 1930, made at Orrefors. *Victoria and Albert Museum.*

150   Bowl and bottle, 1948, by Edvin Öhrström, Orrefors. *Orrefors.*

151   Vase, clear glass with engraved lines, c.1946, designed by Tapio Wirkkala, Iitala Glassworks, Finland. *Victoria and Albert Museum.*

152   Vase, 1940, Venini. *Victoria and Albert Museum.*

153   Vase and bowl, Barovier. *Victoria and Albert Museum.*

154   Clear glass with threaded decoration, c.1951, by Archimede Seguso. *Victoria and Albert Museum.*

155   Two-handled vase, rock crystal mounted with enamelled gold, probably Florentine, width 5½ ins, early 17th century. *Sotheby's.*

156   One of a pair of Louis xiv rock crystal table candelabra, height 23 ins. *Christie's.*

157   Block of rock crystal, 25 × 14 × 11 ins. *Sotheby's.*

For

WINIFRED ILLINGWORTH
to remind her of our
expedition to Altare

Preface and Acknowledgements

Everyone who is even sketchily familiar with the intricacies of the history of glass manufacture in Europe will realize that many volumes would be required to treat so vast a subject as it deserves. All that I can hope for from the following pages is that I have managed to preserve a reasonable balance between the distant past and the near present and to treat this magical, flexible material with due respect. Of all the arts of fire the technique of glass-making has done as much as any of the others to lighten man's journey through time. It has provided him with many of the amenities of civilization and also, thanks to the imaginative vision of a few gifted individuals, has left to him many remarkable vessels which have added to the sum total of the world's visual delights. It is the latter, the objects which the French call *'vases de délectation'*, that are the main theme of this book, though the value of the industry to the work-a-day world is not, I trust, forgotten.

No one attempting a survey of this sort within the limits of this book can avoid anticipating the criticism that he has omitted too much. I agree – one could easily find another thousand worth-while illustrations, but whether that would add materially to the reader's edification is another matter. It is so simple to bemuse the enquirer who is not yet at home in the subject by showing him too many objects at once.

My principal sources for this survey were as follows:

W. B. Honey, *Glass: A Handbook and a Guide to the Museum Collection*, Victoria and Albert Museum, 1946

D. B. Harden, K. S. Painter, R. H. Pinder-Wilson, Hugh Tait, *Master-pieces of Glass*, British Museum, 1968

For Bohemian glass I have relied largely upon the Victoria and Albert Museum's illustrated book published in 1965 under that title at the time of their memorable exhibition, with its introduction by Dr Libuše Urešová of the Museum of Industrial Art, Prague.

For the French chapter I have consulted *La Verrerie en France* (1953), an admirably detailed little book by James Barrelet, one of the paperback volumes of the Larousse series *Arts, Styles et Techniques*.

London is fortunate in possessing a superb collection of Spanish glass at the Victoria and Albert Museum and the world in general remains hopelessly in debt to Mrs Alice Frothingham, Curator of Ceramics at the Hispanic Society of America, New York, for her monograph *Spanish Glass* (Faber, 1963). No one can write about Spanish glass without reference to this masterly work, nor is it possible to discuss the glass of the twentieth century without reading and frequently quoting from Mrs Ada Polak's monograph *Modern Glass* (Faber, 1962).

Apart from these sources I must thank many good friends – not least among them the firm of Lobmeyr in Vienna – for advice (and warnings). Owners of individual pieces are gratefully acknowledged in the list of illustrations.

1 Introduction

Every country has its own pride, which sometimes leads to idiocies and can so distort values that we all spend so much energy admiring ourselves that we have no time left to take any interest in our neighbours. In England the story of our own glass industry has been told in dozens of admirable books and in great detail. Innumerable articles and illustrations have sung our praises as innovators and designers so that one may easily express surprise that, after such triumphs extending over so long a period, anyone beyond the North Sea and the Straits of Dover had the heart to continue to produce glass at all in their own manner once George Ravenscroft, towards the end of the seventeenth century, had introduced the use of lead as one of the constituents of this marvellous material. The fact is that while his experiments were immensely important and laid the foundations for the expansion of the industry in England, her neighbours elsewhere were not, on the whole, so impressed and preferred to cling to their old ways and to improve upon them. The basic differences – there are of course innumerable variations – can perhaps be summed up thus. Silica (usually in the form of sand) plus soda plus lime, suitably heated, produces a normal ordinary glass, the proportions being perhaps soda fifteen per cent, lime ten per cent and silica seventy per cent, the remaining five per cent perhaps colouring and purifying materials. The English formula will differ considerably – more like lead oxide thirty per cent, potash eighteen per cent, silica fifty per cent. The mixture of lead and potash gives a softer glass, easier to work.

The metal which we call glass is so remarkable that though by now we take it very much for granted, it still remains something of a mystery and one can still, in spite of precision engineering and scientific control of furnaces, feel something of the awe with which the early seventeenth-century James Howell regarded the manufacture as he saw it on the island of Murano; he reported his visit to his employer Sir Robert Mansell in these words:

The art of glassmaking is here very highly valued, for whatsoever be of that profession are gentlemen *ipso facto*, and it is not without reason, it being a rare kind of knowledge and chymistry to transmute dust and sand (for they are the only main ingredients) to such a diaphanous pellucid, dainty body as you see a Crystal-Glass is. . . . But when I pried into the materials and observed the Furnaces and Calcinations, the transsubstantions, the liquifactions that are incidental to this art, my thoughts are raised to a higher speculation.

A nice man, Howell, displaying a very proper humility before the wonders of science, as he was faced by a material derived from such ordinary constituents, and yet capable of being blown, manipulated, twisted, moulded, engraved; endowed with the quality of transparency, of reflecting light; smooth to the touch, brittle yet tough, one of the marvels of the world, manufactured by men who were clearly possessed of knowledge beyond the ordinary. Magic was not far from the minds of Howell and his like and, reading between the lines, it is not difficult to detect a certain wholesome fear of the mysterious processes which he was unable to understand but which evidently worked. Modern techniques enable glass to be churned out *ad libitum* to identical patterns and so add enormously to the efficiency, convenience and amenities of material civilization; indeed it is next to impossible to imagine the world without it. This aspect of the industry is immensely important, but it is not the immediate concern of this book. What follows is an attempt to trace the rise and fall and renaissance of the craft throughout Europe from Roman times until the day before yesterday, dealing not with the mass-production of glass for the table or for scientific purposes, or with window glass, but with glass vessels of various kinds, the fashioning of which was in each case an adventure, the craftsman, generally anonymous and humble, knowing what he wanted but never quite sure that the final result would be up to his expectations. This was the case for many centuries and still holds good. Many of us consider that that is largely the reason why the study of so extraordinary a metal remains perennially fascinating.

Roman Glass

The chief centres of glass-making before the days of Augustus were Syria and Egypt. It was in the former area that some unknown person, probably by chance, discovered that the molten, viscous metal could be blown into an almost infinite variety of shapes, and so inaugurated a revolution in the fashioning of glass vessels that, within the narrow confines of the craft, is comparable with the invention of the wheel by some equally unknown prehistoric genius. We are concerned here with Europe only, but it must be pointed out at this early stage that there are many cases in which it is still a matter of opinion whether a particular glass found in, say, Cologne was actually made there or was imported from Italy or even from the Near East. What seems to be certain is that both Egyptian and Syrian workers had established themselves in Rome, the centre of the known world, by the first century AD and that they, or their skills, quickly spread as far as Spain and Britain. The most famous of the glass-houses of the West were those of Cologne. These were in operation quite early in the first century AD, to be followed within a hundred years by others in what is now Belgium. A great deal was no doubt imported from the Near East and Egypt, but both areas exported not only their glass but their workers, so that by about the year AD 200 the various strains that go to the making of a local style were more or less fused together; thus throughout the whole extent of the Roman Empire it was possible to recognize a common stylistic language in the glass produced for ordinary use. The general standard was high, but there were evidently glass-workers who could go far beyond the normal skilful manipulation of the metal and could produce objects of the most extraordinary sophistication. The most convincing evidence for this is to be found in the British Museum, first in the Portland Vase – no doubt the most famous glass in the world – and secondly in the Lycurgus Cup, not nearly so well known though in some respects even more remarkable (figures 1 and 2). No account of Roman glass can be written without describing each of them at some length, even though they have been discussed so much in the past. As is the case with other objects of comparable quality, one can return to them again and again under various conditions of light, and still find they have something fresh to say. I make no excuse, therefore, for referring to them once more. The Portland Vase dates from about the beginning of our era and is said to have been discovered in 1582 in a sarcophagus on the Appian Way near Rome. It was first recorded in 1642, by which time it was in the Barbarini Palace in Rome itself. Sir William Hamilton, our man at Naples, later the easy-going husband of Nelson's Emma – his Greek vases are an important part of the British Museum collection – brought it to England, and in 1785 sold it to the Duchess of Portland. The fourth Duke of Portland deposited it on loan in the British Museum in 1810. In 1845 it was smashed by a lunatic with a grievance, but repaired with extraordinary skill; it was offered for sale at Christie's in 1929. Sir William Hamilton had sold it to the Duchess for the then staggering price of 1,800 guineas; it was now bought in for 29,000 guineas. Eventually in 1945 it was purchased by the museum. The vase is an amphora of cobalt-blue glass cased with opaque white, in which the design is cut cameo-fashion in relief. The technique involved first blowing the vase and then dipping it in the opaque white, with the danger of the outer casing cooling too fast and breaking the whole vessel; then came the no less delicate operation of cutting the outer casing just so far and no farther so as to reveal the figures in low relief against the blue background. This cutting and grinding is so carefully carried out that, where the design demands it, the white casing is so thin that the blue background appears as a mere faint shadow through the white. The subject thus depicted has aroused a good deal of controversy in the past as to detail, but there seems to be general agreement now that it represents the story of Peleus and Thetis, the parents of Achilles.

The Lycurgus Cup (figure 2) is one of those strange objects which is almost impossible to illustrate because, though it is opaque green on the surface, it becomes wine-coloured when viewed by transmitted light. In addition there are subtle variations in certain portions – a patch for instance where the surface colour is yellower than elsewhere and, in transmitted light, transparent amethystine purple. Analysis has shown that the glass contains minute percentages of manganese and gold, the former, it is thought, contributing to its reddish purple colour, the latter to its strange optical properties. Apart from this, which may be considered a chance oddity rather than an extraordinary beauty, the cup remains an outstanding example of cutting and grinding in high relief and finally polishing to a glossy finish. The design shows Lycurgus held captive by a vine, while Pan is egged on to attack him by Dionysus accompanied by his panther; a satyr prepares to hurl a rock with the nymph Ambrosia reclining at his feet. The story is that of the Thracian king Lycurgus, who was so unwise as to object to Dionysus and his followers. One of them, Ambrosia, fought off his attack and as he tried to smash her skull, prayed to Mother Earth to save her. Earth heard and Ambrosia sank down, changing into a vine which trapped the king.

So much for the two most remarkable of the Roman glass vessels which have come down to us. But these, of course, were objects of great luxury, the kind of thing perhaps which, according to Pliny (AD 23–79), Petronius smashed so that it should not fall into the hands of the Emperor Nero – the gesture of the true connoisseur hating the thought that a thing of beauty should belong to someone who would inevitably fail to appreciate it as it deserved. Once the blowing technique had caught on the way was open for the manufacture of innumerable utilitarian vessels – jars for the storage and transport of wine and oil, bottles for perfume, ointments and medicines, drinking glasses, lamps, plates and dishes. Such things have survived in considerable quantity in spite of their fragile nature and their near paper-thinness. The craft was at last freed from its age-old dependence upon ceramic traditions and could branch out on its own. Moulding was of course still necessary for certain shapes: for the delightful *Bonus Eventus* plaque, for instance (figure 3), which, like the two previous pieces, is also an admirable example of cutting. Moulding was used in conjunction with blowing, but it was the latter method that gave the industry its flexibility. Shapes are

5

frequently of wonderful purity, with a minimum of adornment and – in twentieth-century eyes – much enhanced by the purely fortuitous results of long burial in damp soil. This has resulted in surface decay (occasionally deep-seated) and in a most attractive rainbow iridescence. If the piece is immersed in water, which will fill the interstices of the laminations, this colouring vanishes, but reappears as the vessel dries. There are a few examples of enamel painting and also fragments of so-called gold glasses – that is gold-leaf laid upon a small disc of glass and engraved and then protected by a second layer of glass placed over it. Nearly two thousand years later a Paris picture-frame maker made use of a similar method to add interest to his frames; his name was Glomy and so the word *eglomisé* was added to the language. In Bohemia and the German-speaking lands glass decorated in this manner was known as *Zwischengoldglas*.

Inevitably some shapes can be traced back to their pottery ancestors and a few seem to have been derived from silver vessels. Among the noblest and simplest are such graceful objects as the flask seen in figure 4; it was found in Cyprus and was made of greenish glass, the body applied with three winding snake coils, in the late second century AD; or the bluish-green flagon of figure 5 with its seventeen spiral ribs, from the third quarter of the first century AD, found in the cemetery at Barnwell in Cambridgeshire; or the two-handled wine-coloured jar of figure 6, first century AD, from Campania, Italy; and the fourth century AD bowl from Cyprus in figure 7, which is nearly colourless but has a faint green tinge with dark blue blobs. The rectangular bottle in figure 8, bluish-green, of the first or second centuries AD, was found near Faversham in Kent during excavations for the London, Chatham and Dover Railway and is an admirable and intact example of a type which was no doubt pro-duced in considerable quantities. The ribbed bowl of figure 9, ascribed to the third century AD, bluish-green, also came from the Faversham site, while the two ribbed flagons in figures 10 and 11 were found at Bayford in Kent, one being olive-green with two handles, from late first or early second century, the other bluish-green, from perhaps a century later. The jug of figure 12, of the fourth century AD, comes from Andernach in Germany, the facet-cut bowl of figure 13, from the second century AD, was also unearthed in Germany, from a grave at Leuna-Merseburg; it has three rows of vertical oval facets, then a wheel-cut, a band of circles with their central knobs in sunken relief, and three more lines of oval facets, and is therefore an intact example of blowing and cutting.

A few – a very few – individual names have survived. One is that of Ennion, a first century AD maker whose name appears on mould-blown glass of the period, and who is believed to have begun with a workshop in Sidon and later established himself in Italy. Another is Frontinus, whose glass-works flourished in the third and fourth centuries at Boulogne or Amiens. If it is possible to sum up the achievements of the glass-workers during the first four centuries of our era, before Rome collapsed under barbarian pressure, one can say that they were in remarkably complete command of the processes which later centuries developed and extended – they cut and engraved, they decorated in gilt and enamels, they made use of blowing and of moulding, sometimes separately, sometimes in combination and, in general, set standards which Europe had to rediscover with much toil and trouble.

2 The Twilight of Rome

When, at about the beginning of the fifth century, the lights began to go out all over Europe (as they have more than once since) the skills remained but the markets disappeared. The change was no doubt gradual and, taken by and large, undramatic, but it was there none the less; this was an altogether simpler, rougher age, and the narrowness of the range of the glass objects which have survived is marked. There is no painting, nor any of the several varieties of cutting; mould-blowing survived, but only for easy, ordinary patterns, and the only other pleasant trick from the past was trailing, by which a linear pattern was 'trailed' over the body of the glass vessel. The best thing of these centuries – at least that is how it often appears in the eyes of a millennium and a half later – was the use of prunts or claws, which are seen to great advantage in a series of claw-beakers that seem to have been in favour from the late fifth or early sixth century until the eighth century; they are fine things by any standard.

Figure 14 shows a famous example found in 1775 as the sole object buried with a skeleton at Castle Eden, Co. Durham. It is green with royal blue trails at neck and base and on the upper row of claws. The method of working, after the glass had been formed by blowing, was, according to the catalogue of the British Museum's exhibition 'Masterpieces of Glass', held in 1968, 'trails drawn on, base finished and vessel allowed to cool while held on blowpipe; heated blobs then applied, one by one, for each claw, which warmed part of the wall, enabling the claw to be blown hollow and drawn out into position with pincers; vessel then transferred to pontil for finishing of rim.' In short, this was a type of glass demanding a considerable degree of

8

manipulative skill of which glass workers of Murano a thousand years later would not have been ashamed.

This is just one object out of the nine chosen to represent these centuries in the Masterpieces of Glass Exhibition held at the British Museum in 1968; the nine constituted as notable an array of the achievements of this age of decline as can be imagined. One is left with the feeling that skill was in no way lacking and that the traditions of more prosperous days were still very strong. What was not to be found was a public able to appreciate the finer points of glass manufacture. Europe had to wait several centuries before political and general conditions made it possible for this noble craft to re-emerge from chaos.

Italy

From the Middle Ages onwards the fame of Venice has inevitably shouted down the claims of other centres, of which there must have been many slowly emerging from Dark Age chaos. The place became so famous as the fount and origin of everything either noble or entertaining in the world of glass, especially from the closing years of the fifteenth century until the end of the seventeenth, that it savours of heresy to head this section 'Italy' rather than 'Venice'.

There were glass furnaces in Venice by the eleventh century, and by the thirteenth the danger from fires, as the city slowly rose from the waters, became so great that the government took fright and banished the industry to the island of Murano where, with certain ups and downs, it has prospered ever since; it still remains a tourist attraction of absorbing interest. No one has yet succeeded in identifying any surviving glass as having been made in Venice before the end of the fifteenth century, but a range of fairly simple goblets and decanter-shaped bottles can occasionally be seen in early paintings. The Venetian archives are voluminous and leave historians in no doubt as to the importance of the glass industry to the State which, as time passed, made repeated efforts to prevent workpeople leaving and so revealing the secrets of what had become an immensely profitable trade. Penalties were severe, but in spite of most repressive

9

legislation – there are some unpleasant parallels in modern dictator-
ships – good craftsmen did occasionally escape, some to other centres
in Italy, others north to Bohemia and the Tyrol, yet others farther
still to Antwerp and so, in due course, to England. There is a
considerable difference of opinion as to whether the Venetian glass-
workers were more indebted to the long tradition of the Levant and
Alexandria than to what remained of Roman know-how, which
could not have perished entirely during the slow run-down of the
Empire; the point is not in fact of any great importance. It is,
however, difficult to discount the facts of Venetian contacts with the
last three centuries of the Byzantine Empire, and still more difficult
to imagine that some Christian glass-workers had not found a refuge
in Venice by the time the Turks became masters of Constantinople
in 1453. Whatever the various strands which went towards its
development, the rise of the Venetian industry at Murano gave the
place the lead in the whole of Europe for the manufacture of the
finer sort of glass, so that '*façon de Venise*' became a convenient phrase
with which to describe any glass made anywhere which was not
run-of-the-mill forest glass.

There were inevitably other centres among the numerous medieval
states of the peninsula – Brescia, for instance, and Ferrara – but, in
general, and with one puzzling exception, all paid some sort of
homage to the glass-houses at Murano. The orthodox view is well
summarized by Giovanni Mariacher in his *Italian Blown Glass* (1961):

The diffusions of forms, learned and imitated from those of Murano,
reached such proportions at one time that it is occasionally difficult to
distinguish the objects which originated from the glass houses of the
Lagoon from the copies made beyond the Alps. The difficulty is intensified
by the fact that, at least in the early stages, these articles were often the
handiwork of expatriate Murano craftsmen. A great many names, some
of them belonging to the most famous glass-making families of Murano,
are recorded in documents or other written sources as having worked in
the various countries, thus fostering the development of an industry which
was destined one day to offer formidable competition to that of Venice.

While one can accept this general statement as substantially correct,
it is possible to take the view that it overstates the case. Murano was

important – immensely important – but there is both a living tradition and a certain amount of documentary evidence to show that at least one other centre, now of no great consequence, played a notable part during the Middle Ages and the Renaissance in preserving the knowledge of glass-making and, what is perhaps even more surprising, in spreading that knowledge abroad. It is fascinating to drive from Genoa to the small village of Altare just off the road to Turin a few miles north of Savona and to find there not just a glass-house in operation but a confident pride in the history of the industry in what, in medieval times, must have been a very remote locality by the Cadibona mountain pass, the border between the Maritime Alps and the Ligurian Appennines.

Enquiries at the local garage produced an instant response: 'Yes, there has always been a glass-house here, founded by the Saracens.' My companion and I took this information with several grains of salt, remembering though that immigrants from the Eastern Mediterranean might have found a refuge and a livelihood here and that, to the villagers, all such strangers would be classed as Saracens. English writers, both Honey and Haynes for instance, have spoken of the Altarists as coming from Normandy or Provence or as 'Semites'. In short, though every book refers to the Altarists as important to the history of the industry, no one is able to explain in what manner or in what degree, and no one so far has been able to point to a single specimen of early glass and identify it with certainty as having been made at Altare. Just one piece in the Victoria and Albert Museum, a dish, is very tentatively and half-heartedly assigned to the village on the ground that it bears the arms of Visconti and Riario of neighbouring Savona. A visit to the glass-house a few yards down the main street left us in no doubt whatever about the strength of the tradition as understood by the men actually engaged in glass manufacture today. They are descendants of seven families who, we were informed by one of them, Signor Walter Bordoni (the Italianate form of Bourdon), came to Altare about the year 1000 from Flanders, attracted by the abundance of wood in the neighbouring valleys and the lower slopes of the mountains, and also possibly by the fact that there were French monks in an isolated monastery at

Bergeggi about ten kilometres from Savona. The possibility that these seven families came from either Normandy or Provence was brushed aside without hesitation; they were from Flanders and the story of a Provençal or Norman origin was perhaps due to the fact that the monks were French and not Flemish. The seven families are as follows:

Bormiol (*now* Bormioli)   Bousson (*now* Buzzone)
Bréaund (*now* Brondi)   Saroud (*now* Saroldi)
Bourdon (*now* Bordoni   Blanchard (*now* Biancardi)
    and Bordone)   Varaud (*now* Varaldi)

Signor Bordoni adds that later members of eight other families came to Altare from Venice – the Marini, Greni, Bertoluzzi, Somaglia, Negri, Mirenghi, Perotto and Vico; a little later still the Lodi and the Massari came, and from all these was formed *L'Università dell'Arte Vitrea*, the Society of the Art of Glass-making. The earliest document, as far as he knows, in which Altare is mentioned dates from 1140, and the earliest in which the name of Altare is connected with glass manufacture from 1282. W.A.Thorpe, in his *English Glass*, has a note which gives a slightly different account, relying on records in the library at Savona:

According to a probable tradition, the Altarist glass makers came from Normandy and Brittany about the 9th century and obtained the *luogo dell'Altare* [just north of Savona] from the Signori di Monferrato in token of their art. They brought with them the glassmanship of Roman and Merovingian Gaul. They were several times ennobled or privileged by the Marchese di Monferrato, notably in 1495 and in 1512; and it was probably about this date that they adopted *cristallo* from Venice. But they continued to work in the Northern code of *Waldglas*, and it was by virtue of this that they were so much employed in Germany and the Netherlands; *Rysselsche nach Art der Altaristen* are mentioned at a Kiel glasshouse in 1655.

He then goes on to a list of nine, not seven families 'of their original noblesse' – the additions are Raquette (Racchetto) and Perrot (Perotto) – and notes that some of them had returned to France at least a century before the Venetian dispersion began. In about the year 1630 the English tycoon Mansell said that he went to great expense to obtain a set of glassmakers from Mantua to replace Venetians who were leaving him. Thorpe thinks (but does not give his reasons) that these replacements were Altarists and that the expense was partly due to the *Consoli Vetrai* who governed the *Università dell'Arte Vitrea del luogo dell'Altare*, and that the families of Da Costa and Dagnia, well-known in the English industry, were also from Altare. Whatever the exact circumstances which led to the establishment of glass-houses at Altare, and in spite of the fact that nothing seems to have survived from what must have been, in the course of years, a considerable output, the influence of the Altarists must have been important, and a good deal more far-reaching than their contemporaries, sheltering behind the hidebound laws of the Serene Republic, would care to admit. The *Università dell'Arte Vitrea* appears to have been exceptionally enlightened and to have raised no objections to its members wandering far from home; in 1495 its policy was codified in a statute that seems to have been made expressly to encourage contacts abroad. The principal beneficiary of this liberal attitude was France, particularly Nevers, whose ducal house was related to the Gonzaga family of Monferrato. Both at Nevers and elsewhere Italian names are prominent, some of which are still to be found at Altare – for instance, Bormiolo, Buzzone, Perotto, Racchetto. We shall never know just how much, or to what extent, the rest of Europe remains in debt both to Venice and to its more modest, less famous and less commercially successful rival. It is worth remembering that in addition to the customary sixteenth-century wording '*à la façon de Venise*' the phrase '*à la façon des Sieurs Altaristes*' also occurs in documents.

Whatever the source of this influence it is reasonably certain that a great deal of glass made by, or as a result of, the instructions given by emigrant Italians was and remains indistinguishable from actual Italian work. National styles hardly began to take shape until the seventeenth century, and one can, with a good conscience, remain sceptical over a too rigid classification of the work performed '*à la façon de Venise*' at centres as far apart as Antwerp, Liège, Cassel, Hall-in-Tyrol, Nuremberg, London, Spain, and at many other places in Italy itself, in France, Bohemia, Belgium and Germany. Craftsmen from Murano were working at Antwerp by 1541; from 1569 onwards Venetian-style glasses were being made at Liège in a glass-house staffed by emigrants from Altare. Liège was a place destined to grow to very real importance as a glass-making centre during the following century under the direction of the Bonhomme family; the Venetian Verzelini reached London from Antwerp in 1571 and obtained a privilege from the Crown four years later to make glasses *à la façon de Venise* and to teach Englishmen the art. One may perhaps sum up the position thus: until the sixteenth century Europe as a whole relied upon the age-old glass-making know-how left over from the decay of the Roman Empire. After that, during about two centuries, more sophisticated techniques were introduced, notably that which enabled the metal to be purified to a near-crystal brilliance, and some very pretty tricks indeed began to be played in manipulating the metal in its viscous state. This sophistication gradually spread all over Europe; the credit must be given to Italy and, at this stage, to Italy alone, irrespective of the claims of this or that particular centre. The details remain obscure, but there is no question as to the brilliance of the performance as a whole. Just how brilliant it was must now be examined.

The glass-houses of Venice on the island of Murano did not of course spring up overnight, nor were Venetian skills acquired without reference to the distant past, whether from traditions handed down on the soil of Italy itself or from contacts with the eastern shores of the Mediterranean. Eleventh-century records show dealings with Alexandria, the great centre of glass manufacture during Roman times and also after the rise of Islam. By the end of the thirteenth century Murano was exporting its products and was importing *verre brizé*, i.e. broken glass, which the English trade knows as 'cullet', from Syria; the term is used in a treaty of 1277 between the Doge Jacopo Contarini and Behomond VII, Prince of Antioch. Nothing of this early production has survived. It is thought that perhaps before the fifteenth century the Venetians may have discovered – or rather rediscovered, for the trick had been lost for centuries – the means of decolourizing glass by the use of manganese, thus achieving a fairly clear transparent metal resembling the much admired rock-crystal. But throughout medieval Europe coloured glass was also popular because of its superficial resemblance to precious stones. Alchemists were encouraged not only to attempt to transmute base metals into gold but to change coloured glass into gems, and there must be few cathedral treasuries in Europe which do not possess some sacred vessel or other or a fine binding which is not adorned in this manner. One of the best known of these is the emerald-green bowl now beautifully displayed in the Treasury of the Cathedral of San Lorenzo in Genoa, long considered to be an emerald and described, at one time and another, as the Holy Grail, a present from Solomon to the Queen of Sheba or the dish which Salome presented to King Herod with the head of St John the Baptist upon it. But this was probably Alexandrian work, and in any case was loot taken at the sack of Caesarea in 1101 by a crusader from Genoa. This is the legendary sacred vessel, for long kept safely out of sight, referred to in a letter from Genoa dated 28 August 1718 from Lady Mary Wortley Montagu to her sister the Countess of Mar: 'The church of St Lawrence is all black and white marble, where is kept that famous plate of a single emerald, which is not now permitted to be handled, since a plot which they say was discovered to throw it on the pavement and break it – a childish piece of malice which they ascribe to the King of Sicily, to be revenged for their refusing to sell it to him.' Similarly there are numerous examples of glass, mounted in Byzantine metalwork for church use, in St Mark's, Venice – plunder, like the bronze horses, from Constantinople in 1204 – but these again are from the East. But though the clear glass was greatly admired and had become the most famous kind of Venetian glass by the close of the sixteenth century, the coloured glass retained its appeal. Blue, green and purple are characteristic and, by the time Antonio Neri wrote his famous treatise on the art of glass-making in 1612, it is likely that the essential formulae were known to many far from Venice. In any case Neri's information came chiefly from his own experience in the glass-works in Antwerp which had been founded and staffed by Venetians. In addition to these one-colour glasses very pretty tricks were played by a mixture of colours designed to imitate onyx, agate and chalcedony, and it was Venice which introduced the so-called *millefiori* patterns, familiar enough to the modern world from thousands of nineteenth-century glass paperweights. A rather later whimsy which must also be credited to Venetian ingenuity was known as aventurine glass, in which metallic particles were scattered over the glass while it was still hot.

Early surviving goblets are clearly based upon similar objects in silver, often enamelled. Tastes will differ, but in my view the finest to be seen in England is the large standing cup and cover in the Felix Slade Bequest at the British Museum, of colourless glass, the bowl ornamented with wrythen gilt ribs, a swirling pattern which is repeated on the cover. The cover is surmounted by a flat-headed knop in which is a partially defaced shield of arms within a blue ring. The stem has vertical gilt ribs and the foot is decorated with intertwined stripes of white and blue enamel and white rings strung together by a red cord while the rim of the cup is enamelled with a white and blue circle and red and blue dots (figure 15). This dates from the second half of the fifteenth century, as does a large, deep bowl, also in colourless glass, with ribbed foot, the bowl itself decorated with a deep band of scale pattern in gold with raised enamel dots (figure 17). Only one degree less noble than the British Museum standing cup and cover is a rather smaller vessel in the Victoria and Albert Museum, sparingly decorated in gilt and with a small pattern of dots round the rim in coloured enamels (figure 16).

Of the enamelled coloured glasses extant which can be confidentially dated to the fifteenth century two are particularly endearing. One of them is the opaque turquoise-blue beaker enamelled with the story of Pyramus and Thisbe, known as the Fairfax Cup, which was sold at Sotheby's in 1959 and went immediately to the Victoria and Albert Museum. The other is a standing cup in the Slade Collection in the British Museum; it is sapphire blue, its stem and foot have raised ribs and are sprinkled with granular gilding (figure 18). The bowl is decorated with a charming procession against a background of clipped trees executed in many-coloured enamels heightened with gold – a triumphal car on which three figures are seated beneath a canopy preceded by two *putti* mounted on a pair of geese; on the other side is Venus seated in a fish-shaped car, which is led forward by Hymen carrying a torch; the car is followed by a centaur ridden by a youth and grasping the hand of a horseman in the armour of the early part of the century. Each of these entrancing glasses betrays a not over-skilful hand: this is part of their charm. By comparison a goblet in the British Museum (Waddesdon Bequest) is far more accomplished – and scarcely as attractive. None the less it is a noble, dignified glass, with an ogee-shaped bowl and ribbed foot with a stem of lapis-lazuli blue. The bowl is enamelled and gilded in a scale pattern and with medallions of a young man and a woman; it is presumably a wedding glass (figure 19).

A certain number of armorial glasses have survived, many of them enamelled with the arms of German families. This has led to a good deal of confusion concerning their origin, but the general opinion seems to be that, such was the fame of Venetian work by the middle of the sixteenth century, the great majority were made and enamelled in Venice to the order of these families. An earlier specimen, un-doubtedly Venetian, is a goblet in the museum at Breslau made for Mathias Corvinus, King of Hungary, who died in 1490. An even rarer type of sixteenth-century decoration is painting on glass in unfired oil colours – a singularly ill-advised procedure, one would have thought, for the colours could hardly be permanent. For a decade or so decorators presumably thought that they could emulate the maiolica painters by covering dishes with all-over designs adapted from prints by Marcantonio Raimondi after Raphael and similar compositions. There appear to be no examples of this ill-judged pictorial extravagance in England, only in Paris, Stuttgart and Berlin. A very pretty trick, also originating in Venice, is the so-called Ice-Glass, which became *à la mode* in the sixteenth century and in due course spread to other European glass-houses, particularly to those in the Netherlands. The characteristic, apparently frosted surface (not to be confused with 'crizzling') is produced by plunging the glass in water while it is still hot and then reheating it at once. But probably the best-known and most admired of the later Venetian glass – popular from the sixteenth century until well into the eighteenth century – is *latticino* or *latticinio*, in which white or coloured threads of opaque glass are embedded in the material. Honey described the method thus:

Rods enclosing straight or spirally arranged threads of white glass were arranged with others round the sides of a cylindrical pot and then taken up on a small gathering of clear glass; by twisting the gathering or the rod formed by drawing it out, simple or complicated crossing and inter-lacing patterns were formed in the glass, which was subsequently blown and manipulated in the usual manner. . . . Glass with the more intricate patterns of this kind is known as *vetro de trina* or lace-glass.

All down-to-earth technical processes, accurately described, appear simple commonsense, in much the same way as a mathematical description of the methods used by a first-class international golfer to achieve his astounding accuracy would appear to be within the reach of everyone. As most of us have discovered for ourselves, that is not the case, and the graceful miracles of the finest *latticino* glass from the Murano glass-houses owe their virtues at least as much to the personal skill of the operator as to the know-how he inherited from the past and to the experiments he himself made. There is no substitute for skill, for the sensitivity of hand and eye, and for the feel for the hot, viscous metal, for the exact moment of time (I almost wrote the moment of truth) when that unformed blob of warm mystery can best be fashioned, caressed and manipulated into a brittle, comely object reflecting light and ravishing the onlooker. Dating is more than ordinarily difficult, for the method was fashionable for at least two centuries. The general rule is that the more complicated glasses are latish. Here, as indeed in so many instances, the enquirer (if he can remain untouched by preconceived ideas) finds himself puzzled by the apparently impossible problem of deciding whether such and such a piece is by a Venetian working on the island of Murano or by that same Venetian, or his brother or cousin, who had escaped to seek his fortune at Antwerp or elsewhere. It is a problem which exasperates the tidy-minded and is likely to remain exasperating until doomsday.

The opaque white glass used for this *latticino* work bears an obvious resemblance to porcelain and when this last marvellous substance first reached Europe many attempts were made to imitate it. The most successful of these attempts were begun in the second half of the sixteenth century in Florence, when a very beautiful, delicate, fragile soft-paste porcelain, based it would seem upon a proportion of glassy materials – the so-called Medici porcelain – was produced for a brief period, but the process proved too difficult and too expensive. Only fifty-six pieces are recorded. Europe had to wait until the early eighteenth century before true, that is, hard-paste, porcelain was manufactured at Meissen. But meanwhile milk-white opaque glass was a passable substitute, and there is a record of experiments as early as 1470 by the Venetian Antonio di S.Simone. Nothing has survived that can be attributed to him, but there are a few specimens in existence which, on the grounds of style, are dated to the last years of the fifteenth century, and yet others which are attributed to the sixteenth century; but the great days of this type of glass were reserved for the eighteenth century both in Venice and elsewhere. An admirable example of this opaque white glass painted in the manner of porcelain is the well-known plate in the British Museum, decorated with a view of the Grand Canal; with other plates of the series, it was brought back to England by Horace Walpole in 1743 (figure 20). As the views include the Church of S.Simeone Piccolo, which was finished in 1738, one is able to date the series with reasonable accuracy.

Students of English glass will have no difficulty in calling to mind several engaging specimens from the Bristol and Stourbridge glass-houses – beakers, tea-caddies etc. – clearly intended to imitate porcelain. There are a few Venetian glasses in existence which are decorated with diamond-engraving, but it would seem that this method, used with such pleasant results in England and elsewhere, particularly Holland, was not very much to the taste of the Italians; this was partly perhaps because the rather horny texture of Venetian glass was not particularly suitable for this treatment, more probably because of a bias towards colour and manipulative ingenuity as so frequently found in the stems both of Italian glasses and of those made elsewhere but obviously influenced by Venetian fashions.

There is no question of the extent and abiding popularity of these fashions, at least until the close of the seventeenth century. Though there are national styles – or at least styles which can be loosely termed national – the debt every country owes to Italy during the two centuries she dominated the market for the finer sort of glass is enormous. What is next to impossible is to be quite certain just how many of the surviving *façon de Venise* glasses are Spanish or French or Netherlandish or from some other centre. One suspects that national pride has in many instances staked a claim on shaky evidence.

If the glass of Venice was not very suitable for engraving it was still less adapted for cutting, but the fashion for this mode of decoration was well established throughout Europe by the middle of the eighteenth century and Italian glass-makers were compelled to follow suit. As early as 1736 Briati, better known for his milk-white opaque glass, was given a ten-year privilege for the manufacture of glass in the Bohemian style – he died in 1772. The great glass chandeliers of this century – white, milk-white and coloured – were frequently decorated by engraving and, of necessity, by cutting; so were mirror-frames composed of a profusion of flowers, mostly of pink and opaque white glass. Mirrors, though no part of this book, must be mentioned. They were of the greatest importance in the history of the glass industry and Venice was fortunate enough to keep what amounted to a monopoly throughout the whole of the sixteenth century until the close of the seventeenth.

Three specimens of this opaque white glass are illustrated in figures 21 to 23; the earliest, presumably from the seventeenth century, is the two-handled vase of figure 21 from the Victoria and Albert Museum. Figure 22, from the same collection, is a covered beaker painted with a rural scene in brownish red. The bottle of figure 23, from the British Museum, is dated 1747. A coat of arms is enamelled on the neck, on the bowl a woman (perhaps Charity) and three children.

Diamond-point engraving on Italian glass is very rare; when it does occur on early pieces, in a happy partnership with other types of ornament, it is uncommonly distinguished, as the *tazza* from the British Museum bears witness (figure 24). It is from early in the seventeenth century – colourless glass, flat, but with the rim slightly upturned and with a low trumpet-shaped foot. In the centre a chain of blue glass is enclosed between two milled thread circles, the wide rim diamond-point engraved with a floral wreath and two birds. As is so often the case, there is another theory about this *tazza* – that it is not Venetian, but Spanish; this theory, as yet not accepted by everyone, says that the chain motif in blue glass and the diamond-point engraving of floral sprays and birds point to a Barcelona workshop.

Expert opinion is uncertain about the late-sixteenth-century goblet of figure 25; does it come from Venice or from the southern Netherlands where so many Venetian workpeople had settled at that time? It is in any case highly accomplished work, demanding great manipulative skill. It is colourless glass with two raised bands of *latticino* below the rim and beneath them a network of applied *latticino* canes. The knop and foot are carried out in the intricate pattern known as *vetro de trina* or lace-glass.

One could, I suppose, argue about the origin of at least one of the fine glasses of figure 26, which all three appeared in a sale at Christie's; the goblet on the left has, to some eyes, a certain Spanish opulence about it. However, the balance of opinion favours Venice. It is an important goblet with an elaborately grooved spreading foot and enamelled in blue, white, red and gold and dates from the late fifteenth century. The less extravagant goblet in the centre is clear glass decorated beneath the rim with white, blue and gold dots – it is early sixteenth-century – while the tall cup and cover on the right, of the same period, is yet another vessel enriched with delicate diamond-point engraving.

With the remaining illustrations there is no argument. The earliest of them is figure 27, attributed to the mid-fifteenth century, a noble vessel with a hollow spreading foot with a dark blue border, the bowl gadrooned, its rim enriched by two blue threads.

Figure 28 is a sixteenth-century example of the Venetian glass-worker's pretty manipulative tricks with his submissive material. It is a *nef* (ship) to ornament the centre of a table and to amuse children of all ages from womb to tomb – a lively and amusing rival to the handsome silver and silver-gilt *nefs* which graced the tables of the best people in medieval and Renaissance Europe, the best of them the well-known Burghley *Nef*, in the Victoria and Albert Museum; it is borne on the back of a delectable mermaid and Tristram and Iseult can be seen playing chess on their voyage from Ireland.

No less light-hearted but in a different manner is the late sixteenth-century colourless goblet of figure 29, enamelled with three masquerade personages, characters from the *Commedia dell'Arte*, Pantaloon, Harlequin and the Doctor. The former is fighting Harlequin (sword *versus* cut-down stick) while the Doctor tries to make peace.

The three pieces in figure 30 are less obviously elaborate than some of those dealt with previously, but typical of the standards of the sixteenth century. The one on the left is a *tazza*, its *latticino* pattern radiating from a central boss – a spiral network of austere, compelling beauty. The small bowl in the centre has a moulded ribbed base and above that appear small floral ornaments in pale blue, white and gold enamels. The one on the right is a second *tazza* decorated with blue and red dots.

As a contrast, there is the bottle of figure 31, of the seventeenth century, the details of which are a little difficult to distinguish; it is moulded with a band of two lions and two double-headed eagles, the most striking thing about it being the swirling bands of *latticino*; it is a *tour de force*, but, to most modern eyes, too clever by half, a criticism that can be levelled at a great many glass-houses, and not only in Italy, where enthusiasm has been allowed to outrun discretion.

3 Spain

Some indication of the comparative rarity of Spanish glass of high quality is provided by the catalogue of the Walter F.Smith Collection, which was sent over from Rhode Island to be sold at Sotheby's in 1967 and 1968. Out of 1,032 lots, 174 were of continental glass; but of these only three were Spanish, and of these three one was a probable, not a certainty. London though is fortunate, thanks chiefly to the far-sighted acquisition by the Victoria and Albert Museum as long ago as 1873 of a breath-taking series of joyously decorated sixteenth-century glass vessels from Andalusia, most of it bought from Senor Juan F.Riano. This collection can vie with any other in the world, and also includes numerous pieces from the eighteenth-century royal factory at La Granja. There are others in the British Museum and at Glasgow; the Museum of Industrial Art at Prague has a fine collection, most of it from Catalonia, the Hermitage Museum at Leningrad about one hundred and fifty examples, and many belong to the Hispanic Society of America. In Spain itself, where there has naturally been the greatest interest, and where the finer glasses have been treasured by many families whose ancestors acquired them as they came from the glass-houses, there are admirable public collections in Madrid and Barcelona and in several smaller museums, notably that which houses the Mateu collection at Peralada.

At first sight most people, coming new to the subject, may find it difficult to distinguish between Spanish and Venetian glasses – and indeed there are many which are borderline cases – but after a little time one senses rather than sees a subtle difference, something next to impossible to put into words, which leaves one in little doubt about the Spanishness or otherwise of any given glass one happens to be studying. To take a more obvious analogy, once a man has acquired a certain modest knowledge of European painting, he cannot possibly mistake a tapestry design by Goya as anything but what it is – Spanish. The fact that it is possible to argue at some length about certain probably Spanish, but possibly Venetian, glasses is due to the stylistic influence of the Venetian tradition throughout Europe, which was embodied by dozens of anonymous glass-workers, not necessarily Spaniards, but working in Spain. One has the same difficulty with many Netherlandish and English *façon de Venise* glasses. Were they made by Italians in Antwerp? By Italians in London? By Flemings or Englishmen, pupils of the aforesaid Italians? Or what? Spain, of course, as a Roman province, shared in Roman glass know-how, and suffered, no less than Rome, from the barbarian invasions. In her case she was occupied first by Visigoths, but then her history goes off at a tangent. Italy was invaded from the north, Spain from beyond the Pyrenees; but for Spain worse was to come, for the Muslims crossed over from Africa in 711 and were not finally driven out for seven centuries. The fact that, at the peak of their power, the city of Cordoba could claim to be the noblest and most civilized of all the capitals of Europe was no genuine compensation for the imposition of a regime which, by turns mild and tyrannical, was too remote from the spirit of the inhabitants to leave more than superficial traces. But it was, none the less, a close-run thing. The invaders crossed the Pyrenees into France, and had it not been for Charles Martel and the great fight at Poitiers in 732 they might well have dominated all Europe, as Edward Gibbon, in a fine burst of rhetoric, so neatly pointed out in a famous passage:

The tutelar saints, Hilary of Poitiers and Martin of Tours, forgot their miraculous powers in defence of their own sepulchres. A victorious line of march had been prolonged above a thousand miles from the rock of Gibraltar to the banks of the Loire; the repetition of an equal space would have carried the Saracens to the confines of Poland and the Highlands of Scotland; the Rhine is not more impassable than the Nile or Euphrates, and the Arabian fleet might have sailed without a naval combat into the mouth of the Thames. Perhaps the interpretation of the Koran would now be taught in the schools of Oxford, and her pulpits might demonstrate to a circumcised people the sanctity and truth of the revelation of Mohammed.

A long time ago all this, but yet some trace of Islamic stylistic conventions is to be found down the centuries; certain glass forms occasionally echo half-forgotten decorative motifs from the Near East to remind one that the Iberian peninsula, while influenced by Europe, has never been wholly part of it.

By the close of the fifteenth century it becomes clear from documentary evidence that the glass manufactured at Barcelona was known and admired far from Spain – in Rome itself. Inventories speak of colours – blue, purple, tawny-yellow and white (uncoloured and transparent) – and also of variegated colours imitating chalcedony. One entry refers to Moorish-type painting without describing it in detail. Presumably this means enamelled glass imitating importations from the Levant, but it is noticeable that while the earlier lists speak of both Islamic glass and the Catalan imitations of it in about equal numbers, by about 1450 glass made in Catalonia alone takes the place of Near Eastern imports or imitations. Workers from Barcelona set up in the island of Mallorca, and here too there is also documentary evidence, as when in 1453 the city council of Palma drew up a list to combat excessive prices. This notes various shapes, identical with those on the mainland, decanters shaped 'like those of Barcelona' and blown from transparent, colourless glass, high-stemmed goblets which were equally valuable, and certain vases set down as having been made of ordinary glass with a yellowish tint. Allowing for a proper pride in a flourishing industry on the part of the Spaniards themselves, we can, with the hindsight given to us by the passing of about four centuries, go a long way – or at least some of the way – with the sixteenth-century writer who claimed: 'The glass that today is made in Venice is considered excellent but . . . in many ways, that made in Barcelona and other parts of Cataluña is better . . . and so Cataluña is praised and esteemed for its glass, and boxes are shipped to Castilla, the West Indies; France, Italy and elsewhere.' Thus Père

Gil, while others claimed that it was exported to Venice itself; this theory is possible, but scarcely probable.

Other documentary evidence throughout the sixteenth century and the few – very few – surviving specimens testify to the excellence of this glass from Barcelona. For this, and indeed for every detail of the story, English-speaking students are in debt to Mrs Alice Frothingham, Curator of Ceramics at the Hispanic Society of America who, thoroughly familiar with Spanish sources and with Spanish art in general, presents in her monograph *Spanish Glass* so lucid a picture of the development of the industry and of the influences which affected it. What follows is based wholly upon her investigations.

In 1503 King Ferdinand sent to Queen Isabella, then living at Alcalá de Henares, one hundred and forty-eight glasses from Barcelona, to join a collection of over two hundred and sixty pieces already there. All these were bequeathed by her to the Cathedral of Granada for the royal chapel. They were still there in 1526, because the Venetian Ambassador to the court of the Emperor Charles v, Andrea Navagero, mentions having seen them, together with her books, medals and tapestries. All the glasses and most of the other bequests have long since disappeared, probably by order of Charles v, who certainly sold her jewels. It is notorious that Charles, by far the most powerful monarch in Europe, had the greatest difficulty in making both ends meet. This collection was described in great detail by Isabella's lady-in-waiting, Violante de Albión, the year it arrived at Alcalá de Henares, and included plates, bowls and trays; jugs for water and wine; covered goblets and wine-glasses; hand-basins and ewers; flower vases and covered jars; wine flasks, salt dishes and cruets; candlesticks and a rose-water sprinkler (the Catalan *almorratxa*). There was glass of various colours, some of it with religious inscriptions, some ornamented with Arabic lettering, painting in white and coloured enamels, some gilt, or blue or purple, some green. Isabella's daughter Juana owned many glasses, some enamelled and gilt or imitating semi-precious stones, a fashion popular in Roman times, and revived by the Venetians in the late fifteenth century. At Juana's death these glasses were described and listed and some of them may well have been purchased by her husband Philippe le Beau, Duke of Burgundy, when he visited a glass-house in the suburbs of Barcelona in 1503.

Other sixteenth-century inventories reveal lavish purchases of Catalonian glass by noble families, while at the same time making it clear that the native glass-houses, whether at Barcelona or elsewhere, had by no means an easy market. The fame of Venice, and the quality of its products, ensured that Spanish makers had to work to high standards. Thus the third Duke of Albuquerque in 1560 owned a rare treasure of glass, the greater part Venetian, but some of it from Barcelona and Cadalso. In 1586 the property of Francisca Ruiz de Castejón included glass from Venice and Florence and also from Barcelona, Figueras, Valencia and Cadalso. In 1599 Diego Fernández de Cordoba, equerry to the king, enjoyed the use of forty-four items of Venetian glass of various types, many made in Castile and over two hundred from Barcelona. With so lively a demand for Venetian glass and the inevitable attempts in other countries to copy it, it is not surprising that Venetian technicians escaped from time to time from the harsh ordinances of the Serene Republic and offered their services elsewhere – in Spain itself and France, and also of course in Antwerp, at that time Spanish territory, whence came the father of English glass-making, Giacomo Verzelini. The names of several of these wanderers who came to Spain have survived, among them Domingo Barovier, a member of one of the best-known glass-making families of Murano, who settled at Palma on the island of Mallorca in 1600 and claimed that he had brought with him the art of making *façon de Venise* 'crystals' (i.e. clear white glasses) and that imports were no longer necessary. Later, in 1608, he moved to the mainland and established a glass-house at El Escorial in Castile.

Previously King Philip II had been an important patron for both Venetian importers and native manufacturers. In 1564 the inventory of his household goods at El Pardo Palace listed 320 Venetian glasses and 263 from Barcelona; and to this his fourth Queen, Anne of Austria, added 300, also from Barcelona. An interesting claim can be made for the glass-workers of Barcelona: that they produced a clear glass – a crystal as it is usually (and erroneously) termed – before the

Venetians. The evidence is not wholly conclusive, but Catalan inventories dating back to 1389 make use of the word '*blanco*' to describe glasses blown from a transparent and nearly colourless metal; by the mid-fifteenth century these 'crystal' glasses from Barcelona were famous and during the sixteenth century Spanish purchasers ordered 'crystal' and not much besides. If it is true that they did, and it is not impossible, it is suggested that this innovation was due to the early use of barilla, derived from plants growing in the salt marshes and containing carbonate of soda and a small amount of lime. The neighbourhood of Alicante was famous for these plants; Venice imported it for her glass-houses on the island of Murano and during the sixteenth and seventeenth centuries it was in demand by glass-workers all over Europe.

By chance the letters of James Howell to his employer Sir Robert Mansell in England have survived. Sir Robert, who succeeded to the industrial empire of Sir Jerome Bowes, had sent Howell on what appears to have been a roving commission to find out all he could about glass-manufacture abroad; the following is an extract from one of his reports, dated 27 March 1621 – and very vivid it is, as is all his correspondence:

I am now . . . come to Alicant[e] the chief Rendezvous I aimed at in Spain, for I am to send hence a Commodity called Barrillia, to Sir Robert Mansel[l], for making of Crystal Glass. . . . This Barrillia is a strange kind of Vegetable, and it grows no where upon the Surface of the Earth in that Perfection, as here: . . . It grows thus, It is a round thick earthy Shrub that bears Berries like Barberries, betwixt blue and green; it lies close to the Ground, and when it is ripe they dig it up by the Roots, and put it together in Cocks, where they leave it to dry many Days like Hay; then they make a Pit of a Fathom deep in the Earth, and with an Instrument like one of our Prongs, they take the Tuffs and put fire to them, and when the Flame comes to the Berries, they melt and dissolve into an Azure Liquor, and fall down into the Pit till it be full; then they dam it up, and some Days after they open it and find this Barrillia Juice turned to a blue Stone, so hard, that it is scarce malleable; it is sold at one hundred Crowns a Tun. . . .

It is clear from this and from other evidence that barilla was held in the highest esteem; moreover, as Mrs Frothingham points out, the method described by Howell is so primitive that one can well believe that it had come down through many generations and could be a survival from the time when the Iberian peninsula was a Roman province.

Southern Spain

So much for Catalonia, with its many glass-centres, Barcelona itself inevitably the most important; by the sixteenth century it was enjoying a fame which extended far beyond the bounds of the Peninsula. In this respect the area seems to have been unique, for neither in Andalusia in the south nor in Castile in the centre of the country did the glass-makers cater for more than a Spanish market. Naturally enough the glass produced in Andalusia was liable to hark back stylistically to the not-so-distant Moorish past; throughout the southern provinces no clear glass was made, and whatever their colour all glasses have small air-bubbles. Colours range from pale greens to dark olive, from brownish-black to amber yellow, and are often used in combination. Thus the neck of a bluish-green vase will be decorated with a brownish-black thread wound round it, and a similar accent of colour is given to handles. There was a fashion for fantastic loops, for many-handled vases, for elaborate trailing, pincered cresting and similar pretty conceits.

Further to the west, in the provinces of Cordoba and Sevilla, the industry developed on different lines. Thanks to the defeat of the Moors between 1236 and 1248 by Ferdinand III of Castile these two regions were cut adrift from Islam; artistic influence now came from Europe, and with the discovery of the New World Sevilla especially became of immense commercial importance as the chief centre of trade with the Indies and attracted glass-men, both technicians and traders, from Flanders and Venice. In the city of Seville the trade established itself in the street called *El Vidrio* ('the glass-maker'). In at least once instance a Spaniard was not too proud to learn from others, for one of them was Juan Rodriguez who, originally from Cadalso, the glass-centre in Castile, had travelled to both Venice and

Barcelona and finally settled in Seville. In 1557 he applied for permission to establish a glass furnace. His sponsors were three glass-blowers and a merchant, who gave evidence that he knew how to prepare green glass, *latticino* glass, *façon de Venise* and other types. Some craftsmen earlier in the century had sailed to New Spain, so that by 1542 the industry near Puebla de los Angeles was flourishing; a report to the Emperor Charles spoke of it as unique in all New Spain and could claim: 'Three kinds of glasses are blown and worked, crystal-white, green and blue, which supply Spaniards and natives of these regions as far as Guatemala and beyond, and the glasses even go to Peru and other countries.' So far though, no glass has yet been identified as having been made in Sevilla. In the seventeenth century Italian glass-blowers from Murano settled in Cadiz and presumably, as elsewhere, made glasses in the Venetian manner. By about 1730 European traders were present in force, all eager to acquire markets in Spain's colonial empire; predominant among them were Germans and Bohemians, who did well with both engraved and enamelled glasses. A tradition, apparently unaccompanied by evidence, asserts that in the seventeenth century both Velasquez and Murillo tried their accomplished hands at painting glass vessels – perhaps locally blown.

Castile

By the sixteenth century Cadalso in the province of Madrid was the best known of several places that made glass in the domains of Ferdinand and Isabella, who had at least one Cadalso glass, a drinking horn, among their table services in the Alcazar of Segovia. In 1530 their chaplain and historian, Marineo from Sicily, noted that the glass made here was far superior to that of other Castilian towns, and throughout the century it is mentioned specifically in inventories. For instance, when Garcilaso de la Vega died in 1536 he owned more than a dozen glasses from Cadalso in addition to thirty from Venice; in 1549 the Countess of Altamira had more than twenty, including flasks as well as Venetian glasses and maiolica from Tuscany. The third Duke of Albuquerque in 1560 left many Venetian, German and Catalan glasses, plus others from Cadalso, among them a decanter of blue glass with milk-white handles and a drinking glass with a blue handle, besides water jugs, brandy kegs and spouted cups. In 1564 much of the more humble domestic equipment for the El Pardo Palace of Philip II came from Cadalso, the table services from Venice and Barcelona.

A Portuguese observer at the court of Philip III at Valladolid in the early years of the seventeenth century was delighted by the beauty and variety of the six glass shops in the city: 'Glasses of the greatest size . . . of all shapes and colours . . . and others . . . for distilling water . . . retorts, and a thousand inventions which here [at Lisbon] we never see, are not very expensive.' Throughout the century Spanish glass-making was stimulated by the arrival of many Italians and Flemings. In 1608 the Venetian Domingo Barovier, uncomfortable at Palma in Mallorca, his first resting-place in Spain, moved to El Escorial. Numerous other wanderers with the requisite know-how followed, either directly from Italy, or by way of Flanders; or else they were Flemings themselves. One of the latter was Dieudonné Lambotte, who closed down the factory at Namur he had inherited and in 1680, sponsored by the Spanish governor of the Netherlands, moved with the tools of his trade and his Flemish workmen first to Madrid and then to near Cadalso.

Towards the end of the seventeenth century fashion began to change: the demand now was not for the airy-fairy fantasies of the Venetian glass-makers, but for the more substantial wheel-engraved and gilded vessels which were the particular pride of the workers of Bohemia and Silesia; the engraving is all the more admirable because it is worked on colourless – or near colourless – crystal. This the Spanish houses were unable to supply, and the industry fell upon evil days; this was in spite of subsidies to a few favoured individuals, notably to Juan de Goyeneche, who, with the help of foreigners with the necessary skills in the manufacture of crystal glass and of wheel-engraving, set up a factory at Nuevo Baztan in 1720; but production there ceased eight years later and the workers were scattered. In 1722 there were three glass factories in operation in Recuenco; a fourth was built and then later bought by Diego Dorado, whose grandsons inherited it in 1787 and endeavoured, with the help of German artisans, to make fine crystals. But this too was not a success, though until the end their glasses were claimed as 'the most beautiful and crystal-clear of any made in Spain'.

The Royal Factory of La Granja De San Ildefonso

We now reach what is in many ways the most interesting of all the Spanish factories: the establishment which a Catalan, Ventura Sit, under the patronage of Queen Isabella Farnese, was permitted to build in the grounds of the palace of La Granja at San Ildefonso. He had left the Nuevo Baztan factory in 1728 and until 1755 was supervisor over the manufacture of plate glass; another department was that producing mirrors, and each had a high reputation in its day. Neither is the concern of this book, nor is that of another section of the plant, which produced lighting fixtures and chandeliers. But there was also a division which made blown crystal, tableware and pieces decorated with engraving, cutting and gilding, notable examples of which were secured among the other parts of the Riano Collection in 1873 by the Victoria and Albert Museum. This section employed many workmen from outside the borders of Spain, several of them Frenchmen and also a highly efficient Swede, Joseph Eder, who was there from 1754 until 1778, perhaps longer. His son Laurence had the task of engraving in the German manner, while another worthy of the factory was a boy from Hanover, Sigsmund Brun, who grew up to supervise the department for making blown crystals and coloured glasses. This was in 1768 and he was still in charge in 1791.

But the place was always run at a loss; it was remote from its sources of supply and also from possible markets, once it was decided to allow the public to purchase glasses which had hitherto been reserved for the Crown. About 1760 a shop was opened in the Puerta del Sol at Madrid, but would-be purchasers found the glass too expensive; progressive lowering of prices during the next few years did not provide an answer, nor did a royal decree in 1762 by which the factory (the Fabrica De Cristales) was granted the exclusive right to sell its products in the city of Madrid and within a radius of twenty leagues round San Ildefonso. An attempt was made to sell a large consignment in New Spain, but by the time the cargo reached Cadiz the Indies fleet had already sailed for Vera Cruz; the glasses were therefore despatched to Havana, but the results were disappointing, fetching only about twenty per cent of the estimate.

None the less production continued, though unprofitably, and two centuries later students of Spanish glass have reason to be grateful to the skilful obstinacy and devotion to their craft of numerous individuals, particularly to the Sigismund Brun already mentioned, for it appears that it was he who discovered a method for firing gilt upon glass, work which, to judge by the several surviving examples in the Victoria and Albert Museum, has lasted exceptionally well. The painting was carried out with a brush dipped in a mixture of gold-leaf ground up with honey; the design would be fixed to the surface by firing at a low temperature in a muffle kiln and then burnished. Sometimes this gilding was used to emphasize engraving – that is, the designs engraved by the wheel would be covered with gilding. Set down baldly like this it sounds gaudy; it is not, but surprisingly restrained. The factory experimented also with coloured glass, opaque-white glass and with enamel paints. Coloured glasses include cobalt, emerald and aquamarine, and the milk-white glass in its day was claimed as 'produced very perfectly and with it are made various pieces imitating the porcelain of Saxony'. The flower painting is exceptionally attractive – garden flowers in pastel shades of rose-pink, apricot, blue, yellow, white, pale green; and the archives note the names of a few artists who worked both for San Ildefonso and for the Royal Porcelain Factory in Madrid, which Charles had moved from Naples in 1759 when he inherited the Spanish throne.

By 1800 the fashion changed to cut glass in the Anglo-Irish manner. Joseph Bonaparte, King of Spain from 1808 until he was turned out by Wellington five years later, made a drastic change in 1809. He considered the age-old system of royal protection inefficient and maintained that it resulted in stagnation; therefore, 'desirous of opening new ways toward national prosperity', he turned over the Real Fabrica De Cristales and its Madrid warehouse and shop to private enterprise, with pensioners to continue to receive their annuities, and all creditors to be paid. After the expulsion of King Joseph, King Ferdinand VII returned to Madrid in 1814 and proceeded to re-establish the factory as an appanage of the Crown; it remained under royal patronage until 1829, when it was rented to a private company.

The vase of figure 32, from sixteenth-century Barcelona, is probably as early as any of those illustrated here and is also a tribute to Venice, for it is enamelled in the Venetian manner and a sufficient explanation of the fame of the Barcelona glass-men at this time. The metal is transparent and uncoloured.

The vase of figure 33, probably very widely known, for it is one of the most striking items in the collection at the Victoria and Albert Museum, is from the same century, probably from the province of Almeria; it is of transparent green glass with pincered decoration and horizontal threading and has four large and four smaller pincered tubular handles. Pincered handles, though not of so elaborate a type, were evidently popular elsewhere, and for many years; they appear, with horizontal threading, on a vase of smoky yellow glass of the seventeenth century (figure 34), and on two eighteenth-century pieces from the same province (figures 35 and 36), the former of green glass with an internal partition (a double cruet), the latter also of green glass, with a quadruple inverted lip. The seventeenth-century *botijo* (figure 37), also from Granada province, displays the same liking for these manipulative tricks; the metal here is yellowish green.

The three vessels of figure 38 were dispersed at Sotheby's from the Walter Smith Collection; they are admirable examples of *façon de Venise* workmanship. The one on the left is confidently ascribed to sixteenth- to seventeenth-century Barcelona; it is of yellowish glass with opaque-white combed decoration. The small jug in the centre, early seventeenth-century, was catalogued as probably from Barcelona; it is a modest charmer with opaque-white strands and a blue handle. Opinion about the origin of the *biberon* on the right was rather more cautious, the verdict being 'perhaps Spanish'; its decoration is composed of opaque-white tape and twisted *latticino*.

The double-handled vase in figure 39, dating from about 1700, is of transparent blue-green glass overlaid with dark brown and has brown handles and threading, while the unusual vessel in figure 40, of about the same date and also of transparent blue-green glass, is an oil lamp.

The jug in figure 41 is from Catalonia and is late sixteenth- or early seventeenth-century; it has a tooled and pincered handle, while the metal is a pale straw colour and frosted – a trick achieved by plunging the piece into cold water while it is still hot. The two eighteenth-century vases in figure 42 are probably from Recuenco, the one on the left being of green glass streaked with brown – once again with pincered handles – while the one on the right is of uncoloured glass of not very good quality with diagonal ribbing. Its neighbour also has this diagonal ribbing, which is not readily distinguishable in a photograph; it is noticeable how insignificant the two handles are in the vase on the right, as if some more robust design had become atrophied while the vase was in the making. Compare these two with the magnificent design of the sixteenth-century glass of figure 33; it is obvious that the early tradition has become emasculated.

The covered vase of figure 43 shows the La Granja glass-house at its unhesitatingly majestic best, the form generous, the metal clear, engraved and fire-gilt; its date is 1775–85, during the long regime of the Hanoverian Brun. The tray of figure 44 is another product of this royal factory; it is crystal glass blown in the mould, engraved and then fire-gilt, and so is the decanter of figure 45 except that it was enamelled after being blown in the mould.

For the next two illustrations I have to thank the Pilkington Museum at St Helen's in Lancashire. Figure 46 is a cruet (*canadella*) from Catalonia, dating from the late sixteenth century; of transparent straw-coloured glass, with opaque-white combing, it has a finial, vermicular collar, and plain lip and foot. The wine-jug in figure 47 of the mid-eighteenth century, is of blue-green glass, its body ribbed and with a spiral trail round the four lips; it is to be compared with the double-handled greenish vase of figure 36. The early sixteenth- or seventeenth-century vase from either Andalusia or Castile, with its noble proportions and absence of fuss (figure 48), is not least among the Spanish glass at South Kensington.

4 The Netherlands

The word 'Netherlands' itself is vague enough, implying the low-lying lands in and around the delta of the Rhine without necessarily attempting a precise geographical definition. For practical purposes it includes what is now Holland and Belgium and the district that was once the appendage of the prince-bishops of Liège. Germany, and more especially the glass industry centred round Cologne, was just over the border, with inevitable close contacts by way of the great river. It is with no surprise therefore that the characteristic German *Roemer* is seen in so many Dutch and Flemish paintings of the seventeenth century, or that the phrase '*Verrerie des Allemands*' occurs in a late seventeenth-century document at Liège (probably referring to *Roemer*). But the chief glass-making centre of the area during the Spanish domination of the sixteenth century was Antwerp, where glass-houses were staffed by Venetian and Altarist craftsmen. It was these men who laid the foundations of a flourishing industry and it was to Antwerp, chiefly through the enterprise of Verzelini, that England owed the beginnings of her own triumphant emergence as a glass-making country.

Venetian influence remained very strong for a lengthy period, even into the eighteenth century; there are, for instance, winged and so-called 'serpent' glasses engraved by Greenwood (Dutch despite his English name) of the late 1720s in the Victoria and Albert Museum; and there is one in the British Museum engraved in 1757 by the German Jacob Sang, a member of a German family of wheel-engravers who advertised in the *Amsterdam Courant* in 1753. Until Venetian fashions swept everything before them the native glass of the Low Countries is indistinguishable from that of the Lower Rhine and there will continue to be differences of opinion as to the origin of many Venetian-type glasses – that is, whether they were made by immigrant Italians at Antwerp or were imports from Venice itself. After Holland achieved its independence from Spain in 1609 several new glass-houses were established, at Rotterdam, Amsterdam, Middelburg and The Hague, but their output appears to have followed the ordinary forms in favour at the time. Italians at Antwerp (runaways from Venice) are recorded as early as 1541, and men from Altare at Liège in 1569; there the Bonhomme family, with several branch factories, can be said to have dominated the industry throughout the seventeenth century and beyond.

Before we consider a series of glasses which are specifically Netherlandish in character it will be as well to discuss a few which are definitely *façon de Venise* but which, for one reason or another, can be considered as having been made in the Low Countries. Possibly best known of them all is the jug of figure 49, with its silver-gilt mounts bearing the London hall-mark for 1548–9. The jug is decorated with broad vertical bands of opaque-white with narrow lines of clear glass between them. This is a style of decoration normally associated with Venice, but the shape is not, nor is it found in sixteenth-century Italian pottery; it is, however, often seen in sixteenth-century pottery from north-eastern Europe and the conclusion seems to be inevitable that this jug was one of the early productions of Italian glass-men, probably at Antwerp. This example is in the British Museum, having been acquired with the Franks Bequest in 1897. Another identical jug with silver-gilt mounts of 1546 has also survived and is now in the London Museum; it bears the enamelled coat of arms of Sir William Parr, uncle of Katherine Parr, Henry VIII's sixth wife. The British Museum jug may be the one mentioned in two inventories of the household goods of Queen Elizabeth I (1559 and 1574). These two jugs are the only continental glass vessels extant which certainly reached England before the middle of the sixteenth century and the fact that each was honoured by silver-gilt mounts is proof enough that they were regarded as extraordinary at the time.

The following six illustrations are all of glasses which are very definitely in the Venetian manner and are all attributed to one or other glass-house in the Netherlands, the earliest among them probably being figures 50 and 51, each from the second half of the sixteenth century. Figure 50, the *tazza* with the saucer-shaped bowl, is supported on a stem composed of three brackets, each decorated with two gilt strawberry prunts above a gilt knop of lions' heads. The rims of both bowl and foot have narrow bands of granular gilding. This is almost certainly from the Antwerp glass-house, as is the 'ice-glass' of figure 51, with its roughened, apparently frozen surface obtained by plunging the hot glass into water for a moment and then reheating it immediately. It was a Venetian trick which became popular in the sixteenth century and so spread northwards. The centre of the beaker is decorated with three large gilt lion-masks with small prunts in between.

Figure 52, with its opaque-white spiral decoration, is close to some Venetian prototype and the same can be said of figure 53 (from the Walter Smith Collection), while the three illustrated together in figure 55 provide eloquent testimony to the hold that the Venetian liking for serpentine stems, which gave such scope for manipulative skill, continued to have upon these northern countries. A British Museum goblet has a bowl and foot of purple glass, its stem being composed of colourless rods enclosing twisted opaque, white and blue threads with pinched colourless glass round the edges; it has been ascribed to Germany rather than to the Netherlands. The three in figure 54 are perhaps a little more likely to provoke differences of opinion, not as to their interest or quality, but as to their place of origin. All three were from the Walter Smith Collection and were dispersed at Sotheby's in 1968; the one on the left, with its yellow, orange and white convoluted stem and pincered blue wings, was catalogued as second half of the seventeenth century and as 'perhaps Netherlands'. It is diamond-engraved with, on one side, a woman in an arbour, and on the other a flower spray. The centre glass has a hollow, winged and pincered stem with blue scrolls, a little out of harmony perhaps with the elegance of the bowl, with its pattern of diamond-engraved sprays of flowers. The third glass, on the right, is thought to be from Liège, its knopped and pincered serpent stem ornamented in blue.

The serpent-stem wine-glass (figure 54) was seen at Sotheby's more recently; it is a more than ordinary rarity because of its inscription, part of which is difficult to decipher. Below the rim is engraved in diamond-point *A Monsieur Gerrard Bernsaw, Marchand à Eluerfeld 1684: le 12 Xbre* and round the foot appears *Monsieur Glaüberg at fait . . . à la Niercke le 12 Xbre 84*; from this one deduces that Herr Bernsaw lived at Elberfeldt, east of Düsseldorf, and that the glass was made by his friend Glauberg at his glass-works at Niercke; but so far Niercke remains unidentified and the glass is tentatively catalogued as German or from the Low Countries. This type of funnel bowl is not often found among *façon de Venise* serpent-stem glasses; the date is also of interest, showing as it does that the fashion was long-lived, for serpent-stem glasses with the exceptions already mentioned are generally attributed to the earlier years of the seventeenth century. It is worth noting that Sang certainly engraved admired seventeenth- or early eighteenth-century glass rather than that of his own time (see figure 76).

With the remaining illustrations we are concerned with glasses which are more obviously from the Netherlands, though even so it is possible to find occasional instances in which a final decision is difficult. The horn, for example, of figure 56, is considered to be from the southern Netherlands and is dated and inscribed in diamond point at the wide end '*1595 21 Julet*', together with an unintelligible inscription in French. At the narrow end of the horn is a silver bell and mount with the legend '*Qui X Tient X Y X Boit X A X 1599*', and then in the middle of the vessel a second diamond-scratched inscription which reads '*Nicoles Coels at beu icy à la santé de PDB*'; this sounds an unusual, endearing personal note of two friends meeting and Nicoles recording the fact that he drank PDB's health out of this horn – the kind of gesture which, a few years previously, would have inspired Montaigne to a wise, leisurely essay. The horn is in colourless glass.

The goblet of figure 57 is of emerald green glass, the heraldic decoration gilt, the baluster stem partially gilt and moulded with masks in relief. The gilded decorations are two coats of arms and, between them, a tree cut down with a new stem springing from its root. The arms are, first, those of Nassau–Orange beneath a coronet, for Philip William, Prince of Orange, who died in 1618; second, the arms of Nassau, as borne by Maurice, Prince of Orange, who died in 1625. The tree was the personal device of Prince Maurice. Above it near the rim appears the motto *Tandem Fit Surculus Arbor* – 'the sucker at length becomes a tree' – to show that Maurice intended to follow in his father's footsteps. Philip William was his half-brother, at whose death he inherited the title. Maurice became *Stadtholder* in 1584 at the age of seventeen and it is presumed that the goblet was made for him after that date, probably not later than 1610.

Another glass which with reasonable confidence can be considered as from the sixteenth century is the *Stangenglas* of figure 58, which is amber-green and pretty obviously comes from some not over-sophisticated forest glass-house. It is very slightly tapered, becoming octagonal and vertically ribbed in the upper part, and is ornamented with two roughly attached spiral bands of milled glass thread.

The next six illustrations, though of various dates and various degrees of excellence, have this in common: they are all *Roemer*, that useful, popular shape found over a wide area both in the Low Countries and in Germany. Figure 59 is the standard type, familiar from still-life paintings throughout the seventeenth century: of greenish glass, it has a cup bowl, cylindrical stem and a narrow spiral foot. The capacity is rather more than one would expect at a casual glance, for the stem, encircled by a series of raspberry prunts, partly decorative but also of practical use in preventing the glass from slipping out of the hand, is an integral part of the bowl.

A variation on this standard theme is seen in figure 60, from the British Museum collection, and cautiously catalogued as 'Germany or Netherlands, seventeenth century'. Like so many other rarities it came from the Slade Collection. The barrel-shaped greenish glass has six circular finger-grips applied horizontally in two rows.

The four *Roemer* which follow are all typically Dutch and all diamond-engraved. Figure 61, from the second quarter of the seventeenth century, is green, its stem ornamented by two staggered rows of large raspberry prunts and the usual coiled foot with a high kick. The bowl is engraved with a half-length portrait of a young man holding a baton and, in a natural flowing hand, the inscription *Noch Leeft Orange* – 'Orange Still Lives'. The young man is almost certainly William II of Orange (1626–50) who in 1641 married Mary, Princess Royal of England, eldest daughter of Charles I. Their son, destined to become William III of England, was born soon after his death in 1650. The inscription therefore suggests that the glass was engraved at this time to commemorate the birth of the Prince and the continuation of the House of Orange.

Of all the diamond-engraved *Roemer* in English collections many will give pride of place to the one in figure 62, which is from the Victoria and Albert Museum, on account of its vigorous, freely drawn, unhesitating calligraphy, a fine flowing script which is as attractive and as decorative as the Kufic characters on some Persian pots. It is unsigned but, because of its similarity to a very few other glasses which bear the signature of Anna Roemers Visscher (1583–1651), is, with due caution, attributed to this highly gifted amateur. Among her rare signed work is a *Roemer* in the Rijksmuseum, Amsterdam; it is dated 1621 and decorated with flowers and a dragonfly. There is a second in the Hamburg Museum dated 1642, with her motto in Greek, Latin and Dutch, and a third, also in the Rijksmuseum, with fruit and insects and an inscription dated 1646. She was clearly a gifted, cultivated person, the first of several Dutch amateurs who indulged in this unusual, difficult and satisfying pursuit. She had a younger sister Maria (1595–1649) working in the same manner and there was also a younger contemporary, Anna Maria von Schurman (1607–78).

The glass of figure 63 is by Willem Mooleyser, whose signature is found on many glasses decorated in this manner, with dates between 1685 and 1697. Another by him, like this 'Dancing Peasants' glass (also in the Victoria and Albert Museum), is engraved with the arms of the United Netherlands and of William III as King of Great Britain and Ireland and with the date 19 April 1689 – that is, eight days after the joint coronation of William and Mary.

Finally, as the last of this group of *Roemer*, there is figure 64, a dignified glass diamond-engraved with the arms of William and the Seven United Provinces and with an exceptionally well-drawn border of various flowers. There is a signature, 'G.V.NES', of whom nothing is known. A goblet with a winged stem dated 1673 and engraved with the arms of William and of the four Dutch provinces is also in the Victoria and Albert Museum. William had been made *Stadtholder* of the four provinces of Holland, Zeeland, Friesland and Groningen in 1672, though the remaining three were still in the hands of Louis xiv.

The fashion for finger-grips of one sort or another, mostly but not invariably in the form of raspberry prunts, was not confined to *Roemer*. Figure 65 is an engaging example from the British Museum, a *Stangenglas*, of the green, coarse forest glass type, with a high bell-shaped foot-base with a folded rim and with six rows of prunts above this and beneath a single milled ring. This is catalogued as Southern Netherlands or Rhineland, sixteenth or seventeenth century, while another *Stangenglas* in the same collection, dark blue green, with spiked, not raspberry prunts, early sixteenth century, is more likely from the Rhineland.

Another type of glass, a beaker with different kinds of finger-grips, four of them the usual circular prunts, the remainder small and rectangular and covering the whole area up to just below the rim, is illustrated in figure 66. The student of glass owes a good deal to the painters of Holland and what is now Belgium. They were of course not in the least concerned to provide him with information, but their delight in painting natural objects and their passion for meticulous detail rendered them admirable, unbiased witnesses as to the facts. They were fascinated by the way light behaved – by the strange manner in which a flat surface, for instance, would appear curved when reflected in a wine-glass – and they were immensely proud of their skill in painting a colourless, transparent material. To accomplish all this they had to look at the various objects they chose – fish, fruit, pewter, silver, glass – with the closest possible attention, with the eye of a camera without the distortion which the camera so easily gives us; and for that reason what they put down on panel or canvas is as near literal truth as can be imagined.

Figure 67, which is by the not at all famous Jacob van Es, is a typical example of the affectionate care with which the painter dealt with his problems, from the velvety sheen on the grapes to the details of the two glasses, the one on the left with a graceful winged stem and a bowl of gradually increasing bulbous sections inevitably making modern man call to mind a Michelin tyre advertisement, the other a graceful, simple goblet with a baluster stem and what the seventeenth-century English described as 'nipt diamond waies' round the base of the bowl.

I return to further, and splendid, examples of diamond engraving, all of them Dutch, but on glass vessels which are neither *Roemer* nor their near relatives. The majestic goblet of figure 68 – simple baluster stem and domed foot, its date about 1660 – can bear comparison as regards its diamond-point calligraphy with the *Roemer* of figure 62, which has been tentatively ascribed to Anna Visscher; it bears the encouraging invitation *Verdryft De Treurighz* – 'Drive out Sadness'. No less distinguished is the bottle of figure 69, both for its admirable form and for the distinction of its fluid, graceful lettering, with appropriate flourishes. The message is also inviting, for it consists of a couplet in praise of wine, paraphrased from the Book of Ecclesiasticus. The engraving is by the amateur Willem Jacobsz van Heemskerk (1613–92), a cloth-merchant of Leyden and also a poet and dramatist; he added engraved decoration with his signature and the date to many glass vessels, mostly bottles, between 1648 and 1690. There is a second one by him in the Victoria and Albert Museum, this time dated 1648, ten years after the one illustrated.

It would be tempting to identify the mounted figure beneath a tree preceded by a musketeer in figure 70 as William of Orange at the age of about twenty (its date is about 1670) but that would be no more than wishful thinking; it is also diamond-engraved and turned up at Christie's in 1966. With the next two glasses we can be definite. The tall flute-glass of figure 71 (a favourite shape in the Low Countries during the seventeenth century) is diamond-engraved, on the one side with the half-length portrait of a young boy wearing a plumed hat and holding a baton, on the other with the coat of arms of the House of Orange, beneath which a sapling is growing from a belt of grass. Beneath the portrait is the inscription '*Wilhelmus Prince d'Orange*'. The short stem is composed of a hollow inverted baluster on a folded foot. The boy appears to be ten or twelve years of age and the glass – if the portrait is of William – dates from the early 1660s.

Nor can there be much argument about the graceful goblet of figure 72, for this must represent Mary, eldest daughter of Charles I of England and Princess of Orange; she married William of Orange when she was nine and he fifteen in 1641 and nine years later, soon after her husband's death, gave birth to the future William III of England. Both bowl and foot are diamond-engraved, the portrait accompanied by an ornate inscription '*Het Welfaren Van De Princes*' ('To the welfare of the Princess'); on the other side is a shield surmounted with a coronet bearing the arms of Orange and England impaled. The only argument about the glass concerns the date when it was engraved. It could have been executed at any time after her marriage in 1641. The inscription makes no reference to the birth of her son and so the general opinion is that it was most probably engraved in 1657–8 when, having attained her full majority, Mary was acknowledged as Regent.

Stipple engraving involves making a design on the glass, still with the aid of the diamond-point, but instead of in lines, in a series of grouped and graded dots, a tedious, delicate method for which the diamond was set in a handle which was very gently struck with a hammer. It is a technique which is today being used with ravishingly subtle effects by Laurence Whistler. At its worst it can result in decidedly niggling designs; at its best, and in gifted hands, it can produce astonishingly ephemeral-looking pictures, permanent of course, but giving the impression that they might fade away at any moment. The man who seems to have set a fashion for this type of work was again an amateur, Frans Greenwood of Rotterdam (1680–1761), who from 1726 was in the employment of the municipality of Dordrecht. It is now, as we reach the eighteenth century, that the majority of Dutch engraved glasses come from England, the heavy English metal having been found more suitable. There is one glass by Greenwood in the Victoria and Albert Museum, its date 1720, which is in line; the museum also possesses three characteristic examples in stipple, one of which shows a toper pointing to a *Roemer* which he holds in his left hand. This is signed 'F.Greenwood 1728'. Another, a glass with a serpent stem signed 'F.G.Fect.' is engraved with a continuous landscape with trees and flowers and a man with two donkeys. Greenwood worked almost entirely from paintings and prints, as did his several followers, among them Aert Schouman, who seems to have stippled glasses mainly as presents for his friends.

There is also an admirable goblet in the British Museum, stipple-engraved by Greenwood with a lively design of Bacchus seated astride a barrel in a woodland clearing accompanied by the customary rout of satyrs, bacchantes, fauns and goats. Beneath a tree is a stone monument on which, also in diamond-point but not of course in stipple, is the following edifying inscription in Dutch – 'The juice of the grape, that delightful sweet thing, Solomon calls a mocker; he who drinks greedily, revels and toasts, will quickly become fuddled and sillier. F.Greenwood made it.' The goblet itself is almost certainly from Newcastle.

The later years of the eighteenth century, as far as engraving on glass is concerned, are bound up with the name of David Wolff (1732–98) who, it is considered, has been credited with the decoration of far more glasses than he could possibly have executed. The engraving in figure 73 is attributed to him; it is a fine goblet, probably from Newcastle, the funnel bowl continuing into a solid stem, the base of the bowl and stem facet-cut giving the effect of a many-petalled flower when viewed through the bottom of the bowl. The design is a rather ponderous allegory: two female figures, one of them holding a scroll inscribed 'Works of the Society K.W.D.A.V.' and on the reverse 'She, who can enchant the Seraphs, who can make tigers listen to her songs; when she plucks the lyre of an Orpheus, Teach Man how Angels sing; Until his song in higher spheres, Unites with that of the Angels'. On the foot is this: 'To the Society; *Art is achieved by Work*, on its twenty-fifth anniversary, on 11 November 1791. The Committee.'

Another glass that is almost certainly by Wolff, though it is not signed, is in the Victoria and Albert Museum; a charmer if ever there was one, it shows two little boys solemnly clasping hands beneath the word 'Friendship' (figure 74). His hand is also seen in the armorial glass in figure 75 which was in a Sotheby sale early in 1970; it is a typical Newcastle glass with a slender, knopped stem, and is engraved with the arms of William v of Orange, son of William iv, and of Anne, daughter of George ii of England. He married Frederica Wilhelmina, niece of Frederick the Great, in 1767.

Jacob Sang has already been mentioned as having worked in Holland; there were three members of the Sang family, which was of Saxon origin, and all were glass-workers. The covered goblet of figure 76 is English glass-of-lead and Sang engraved it on the wheel, signing it in diamond-point on the foot 'Jacob Sang Fec; Amsterdam 1757'. The glass itself is composed of an elaborate figure-of-eight stem with pincered frills. There are 'nipt diamond waies' round the base of the bowl and on the domed cover, the finial repeating on a necessarily smaller scale the design of the stem. The upper part of the bowl is wheel-engraved with a ship named *Velzen* on the stocks and a lengthy inscription, of which the following is a translation:

On the occasion of the hundredth ship, named the Velzen, built by Master Willem Theunisz Blok, in the service of the Honourable East India Company, launched at the yard on 30 June 1757.

The Ship speaks.

Come Artists here, to the IJ,
The Master of the India Company,
The Great Blok, invites you all
And asks all of you what will you have?
First look around me and then inside,
I am Velzen, that enchants every eye:
The hundredth ship this man has built,
Who is not amazed and happy, looking at my perfect shape and line?
He who wants to learn shipbuilding, let him learn here!

As an instance of a successful commercial enterprise making use of the best artistic talent available to celebrate its achievements with dignity and panache this seems to me in every way admirable, and I commend it to the chairmen of our own shipping and ship-building companies.

It has already been noted that Italian glass-workers are recorded at Antwerp in 1541, presumably technicians employed by Van Helmont, who established a factory to make *verre cristallin* in 1537. From then onwards, no less than in France, Italian names are numerous. The Director of the Antwerp factory from 1541 until 1549 was Cornachini. In that year a second glass-house was founded, also in Antwerp, by J.Delamme, who was succeeded in 1557 by Jacques Francisci, followed in 1565 by Jacques Pasquetti and, in due course, in 1580, by Pasquetti's nephew Pedralis. In 1595 Sarah Vinex, widow of a certain Mongarda, took over and in 1598 married Philippe Gridolphi. Meanwhile Francisci – either Jacques or a relative Nicolas – seems to have moved to Liège, which was not yet the great centre of the glass industry it was destined to become; but that venture was a failure by 1571; the following year a new privilege was granted to J.Centurini. One other name, and that not Italian, emerges somewhat dustily from legal records, that of N.de Colnet, who was granted a privilege by Philip II in 1559 and built a glass-house at Barbançon. The name often occurs in documents, mostly protesting against privileges granted to others, but nothing seems to be known about his factory's output beyond the fact that he made ordinary table glass and did not venture to vie with *façon de Venise* importations. Members of the family are recorded as working at Liège, Brussels and elsewhere.

The dominating personality at Antwerp at the turn of the century was evidently Gridolphi. He died in 1625 and from that moment the Antwerp enterprise went steadily downhill. In 1607 he had been granted the exclusive privilege by the Regents, the Archduke Albert and the Archduchess Isabella, sister of Philip II of Spain, both to manufacture and to import Venetian glass. Later he lost the privilege to import, but one is tempted to suggest that, if one can take his own words at their face value, Venetian imports were less of a menace to his business than the competition he had to face from Liège, for he paid Centurini the highest of compliments: 'Liège,' he said, 'imitates Venetian glass so well that the masters themselves can scarcely

distinguish between them.' But the Liège industry still had its teething
troubles and output ceased altogether in 1611. Seven years later the
furnaces were restarted under Guy Libon, who was joined by H.
Ruison in 1624. In 1626 Louis Marius proposed to set up a glass-
house for imitating precious stones, and it is now that we first hear
of Bonhomme, the name which dominates all Belgian glass-making
throughout the remainder of the seventeenth century.

In 1627 Bonhomme takes over and employs Marius. In 1637
Bonhomme's two sons, Leonard and Henri, join the firm. In 1638
they engage two glass-workers from Altare, Jean Castellane and
Guillaume Varaldo; by 1643 they are using coal instead of wood;
by 1660 their interests include furnaces at Liège, Maastricht, Brussels,
Antwerp, Namur and Chatelet; to these they add Verdun in 1664
and Bois-le-Duc in 1669. In 1695 the Bonhomme family is ennobled;
a covered glass with their arms is in the Liège Museum. After 1690
they engage workpeople to make glass *à la façon d'Angleterre*, with
what success is not known, nor to what extent; if they did succeed
in imitating English glass-of-lead as cleverly as Centurini a century
earlier had succeeded in working *à la façon de Venise*, they unwit-
tingly provided yet another problem for later students of the subject.
A curious sideline, which became of considerable importance, was
due to Peter the Great's stay at Spa for the cure, which brought such
fame to Spa water that bottles were specially made for it.

The Bonhomme business declined during the early part of the
eighteenth century, largely because of family disagreements and also
partly because their monopoly was at last challenged by serious competition. This was a new glass-house in a suburb of Liège founded by
Jacques Denis Nizet and Henry Audry, the latter one of the
Bonhomme workmen. The Bonhomme family saw their lawyers
and the resulting legal tangle was never unravelled. The Nizet
concern prospered until 1780 and the Jesuit Felles wrote with
admiration of the remarkable glasses it produced.

In 1727 yet another glass-house was founded, for making wine
bottles and bottles for Spa water; its proprietor was De Grandchamps.
A factory belonging to De Colnet was set up at Namur in 1743 but
was destroyed during the siege of 1746. In 1753 it was re-established

by Sebastien Zoude, at first for ordinary glass and then, in 1762, for what he described as a crystal equal to that of England but a third cheaper. The secret, it seems, was magnesia, but it was thin and not durable and nothing more was heard of it.

Armand Baar, whose *Rétrospective de la Verrerie Artistique Belge* was written in 1930 on the occasion of the exhibition at the *Palais de la Verrerie et de la Céramique* in Liège, sums up the later stages of the industry sadly enough: '*On peut dire qu'au début du XIX siècle, les verreries liégeoises étaient arrêtées*' ('We can say that at the beginning of the nineteenth century the Liège glass-houses were at a standstill'). This means of course that they were concerned only with industrial and day-to-day domestic glass, not with *vases de délectation*.

5 France

The newcomer to the study of European glass will inevitably find himself puzzled by the small quantity of French glass which has survived from the sixteenth century to the end of the eighteenth and, on the whole, by its poor quality. Like other countries, France was the inheritor of the Roman tradition, and during the Middle Ages she was far ahead of the rest of the known world in the production of stained-glass for ecclesiastical purposes; indeed much of it – the windows of Chartres for instance – has long been honoured as among the major wonders of the world. That there was table-glass goes without saying – there is ample documentary evidence – but it was rough forest glass, no better and no worse than that produced elsewhere, and has also disappeared. What is most surprising is to discover that not even in the second half of the seventeenth century, when the ambitions of Louis XIV were so productively linked to the administrative gifts of Colbert, did a new look of any consequence stir the imagination of the dozens of glass manufacturers scattered throughout the country. Saint-Gobain was founded it is true, but for the production of mirror glass to break the monopoly of Venice, and to exploit the invention (of the greatest importance at that time) of the casting of plate-glass; this step forward was due to the patient experiments of Bernard Perrot. The Saint-Gobain factory was established in 1693. Baccarat was not in operation until 1765, Saint-Louis not until 1767; both these subsequently great institutions appear to have owed their foundation to the realization that France was lamentably behind its neighbours in the manufacture of table-glass, for in 1760 the Académie des Sciences offered a prize for suggestions. This is all the more surprising because the France of Louis XIV was setting a standard for the rest of the world in textiles, furniture, silver, faience – all the minor arts – which had an extraordinary influence beyond her borders. The fact remains that, on the whole, French table-glass lags behind its neighbours until the Revolution. We have to wait until the early years of the nineteenth century before the glass from Baccarat and St Louis can vie with that of English or German or Bohemian work, and until the second half of the nineteenth century before the talented Emile Gallé set first France and then the rest of the world on a new course – a subject which will be dealt with at greater length in the chapter devoted to modern glass.

We are so accustomed to take a fine array of glasses on a dining-table for granted that it is as well to be reminded of a custom which was evidently in favour towards the closing years of the eighteenth century and very probably earlier; it might possibly have had some influence in discouraging the production of the better kinds of table-glass. Drinking-glasses do not often appear in representations of eighteenth-century dinner-parties, the more formal ones, that is. The explanation is provided by La Marquise de la Tour du Pin in her *Journal d'une femme de cinquante ans*. Towards 1785, she says, 'Everyone who had a footman decently dressed was served at table by him. There was no carafe, nor a glass on the table. But for great dinners there were silver buckets containing bottles of wine on a side table [*buffet*] with a *verrière* of a dozen glasses and those who wanted a glass of wine of one kind or another would send their own footman for it. He always stood behind his master's chair.' A book on etiquette, both in the edition of 1713 and in that of 1782 confirms this custom: 'Glasses and goblets must be set out on the *buffet* or on a small table covered with a white cloth.'

Although next to nothing remains from so early a period as the thirteenth century (apart from stained window-glass), there must have been a fairly advanced industry in existence if the '*châsse*' mentioned by Marcel Aubert in the Sainte-Chapelle really was made of glass; we do not know the exact shape of this reliquary (such things are normally of Limoges enamel), but if it was of this familiar ark-like shape it does presuppose a glass-making skill far above that of the ordinary forest craftsman. It is thought more likely that it was not made of a single gathering of glass but rather of perhaps six flat pieces fitted into a metal frame.

Glass imitations of precious stones for reliquaries, altar-fronts, vestments, book-bindings were commonplace in France and everywhere else in Europe. It was Charles VI in the fourteenth century who was the first monarch to confirm the glass-makers' privileges as members of the *noblesse*; this of course was not mere snobbery but involved valuable relief from taxation. The earliest document conferring these privileges dates from 1399; in it, Charles VI gives the glass-makers of Mouchamps in Poitou '*les franchises, libertez, droicts, et privilèges desquels usent et joyssent et ont accoustumé de joyr et user les aultres nobles du pays*' ('the exemptions, freedoms, rights and privileges which the other noblemen in the land use and enjoy and are accustomed to use and enjoy'); the pretext is that the profession is by definition ancient and noble – an argument that is repeated three times in the same document. Hence the summing up by Garnier in his *History of Glass* of 1886: 'In France one remained noble although one was a glass-maker, at Venice one was noble because one was a glassmaker and at Altare one was only a glassmaker because one was a nobleman.' All the same, in France he was still, and in spite of royal decrees, not quite a gentleman, for he had to pay for the right to exercise his profession, whereas the gentleman as such did not.

The evidence for glass tableware in the fourteenth century was derived wholly from a few illuminated manuscripts, until 1949, when, during the demolition of the church of the Augustine order at Rouen a wine-glass was found walled up in a niche. The church was built between the years 1390 and 1400. The glass is in the museum at Rouen; it has a domed foot, an exceptionally thin stem and a flower-like bowl, vaguely resembling a tulip, and oddly anticipating Art Nouveau. The type would appear to have been in general use, for it is seen, in the manuscript illustrations, on all kinds of tables, from those of kings and bishops down the social scale to those of ordinary folk.

An amusing sidelight upon the role of the wine-glass in the eyes of the moralists of the day is provided by one illustration which paints the difference between naughtiness and virtue. Two couples are seated at a table; the pair on the left are embracing fervently, the other two conversing quietly; a wine-glass is on the table in front of the baddies, but the goodies are talking happily without one. It is scarcely necessary to add that such glasses, in such constant use from castle to cottage, would be of rough, fragile forest glass. Inventories are another source of information, though it is not easy to identify the shapes of the various vessels mentioned from the Latin or Old French terms used. Some of these lists are formidable; for instance Madame de Savoye orders from Wautier le Lanternier, at Hesdin in the Pas-de-Calais, nine dozen large and six dozen small glasses. The year is 1335.

By the middle of the fifteenth century there were at least twenty-five glass-houses up and down the country and now, for the first time, we begin to read of families destined to make their mark elsewhere than in France, notably four families of Lorraine – Hennezel, Thietry, Thysac and Bisval. The first three, Anglicized, played a notable part in the development of the industry in England. In a document of 1448, renewed in 1469 and 1526, Jean de Calabre, Governor of the duchies of Lorraine and of Bar, granted to these four all the privileges belonging to the nobility: exemption from taxes and subsidies, from military service, from the burden of having troops billeted upon them – all this because of their profession. They have the right of pasturage, of the hunt, of fishing; their products can circulate freely; and these privileges are granted not only to masters but to their workpeople. All this seems to have gone further than the grant by Charles VI already mentioned, and in the following century the Government found it necessary to curtail certain of these privileges, particularly that which gave them a free hand to deplete the forests. Meanwhile the gentlemen glass-makers carried swords and wore embroidered hats and became a hereditary caste.

The first mention of imports from Venice is found in an inventory of 1416 of the Duc de Berry: 'a certain quantity of glasses made at Venice', a rather off-hand item which might be read as implying that they were not worth enumerating or describing in detail. More significant perhaps is the item in an inventory of Charles the Bold in 1467, in which the word *'cristallin'* is used, meaning the clear white glass (not immediately popular, for medieval taste favoured colours) which tradition says was the invention of the glass-maker Beroviero of Murano in 1463. The claim was contested in the early seventeenth century by the d'Azémar family in Normandy, who said that their ancestors in Languedoc two hundred and fifty years previously were the first to make 'crystal', as pure, or nearly pure, white, colourless glass was always called. Rock-crystal had always been admired and therefore it was a high compliment to name a glass 'crystal'. The word was used carelessly enough to indicate almost any near-colourless glass until the nineteenth century when, certainly in France if not always elsewhere, it began to be used with more caution. It could with justice be applied to much of the glass from nineteenth-century Baccarat and to that of Bohemia.

During the sixteenth century Italian influence began to make itself felt in earnest, because the nobility gave its patronage to the products of Venice itself, to the exclusion of the home-made, less accomplished work turned out in great quantity by the glass-houses already established all over France. Leonardo da Vinci, Primaticcio and Benvenuto Cellini were not the only Italians to be attracted across the border. Among the glass-men those from Altare were the earliest arrivals, thanks to the fortuitous circumstance that the Duc de Nevers was related to the Gonzagas, who were the lords of Montferrat north of Savona, in which Altare is situated. It is fascinating, once one realizes how proud the families still working today at Altare are of their French or Flemish origins, to find members of these same families returning to France and, in time, resuming in some cases their French names. Nevers seems to have been the pioneer in thus establishing both masters and workpeople from Altare within its borders, and from there they spread gradually all over the country – to Nantes, Paris, Rouen, Orléans for instance – wherever there was a demand for their exceptional skill. Among the Altarists who, after in some cases five centuries, returned to the land of their ancestors, are the following: Saraldo, Bormiolo, Massaro, Marino, Buzzone, Perotto, Racchetto, Ponta, Bertoluzzi, Ferro and Castellano. There were, as time passed, others from other towns, including a few from Venice itself in spite of the Venetian Republic's attempts to discourage all emigration.

Italians were working at Nantes by 1572, Jean Ferro was making *façon de Venise* glasses there by 1588, other Altarists established a glass-works at Saint-Germain-des-Prés in 1598; they were given a privilege by Henri IV to manufacture glass at Rouen but abandoned the attempt. Things did not always run smoothly, as witness the dispute at Mâcon in 1583. The townspeople objected to the way in which the newcomers were entitled to encroach upon the neighbouring forest and to their exemption from taxes. Moreover, they said that the smoke from the kilns was contagious and encouraged the plague; finally that their products were mere luxuries and of no real use – '*de volupté et plaisir seulement*'. None of these arguments, least of all the last, was likely to appeal to king and court, and it is no surprise to learn that the good people of Mâcon were compelled to bear their afflictions.

Lyons was another important centre where Italians settled, and we have a royal testimonial to the excellence of the work carried out there and at Nevers, in a document of Henri IV of 1597, to the effect that these glass-houses had 'acquired such a reputation for the perfection of their work, that the majority of the glasses of the said crystal, with which our court has been supplied, and everywhere in our kingdom, have come from the said towns of Lyons and Nevers.' High praise this, from the last decade of the sixteenth century, but it merely echoes a similar testimonial nearly half a century earlier from Henry II, who had tried to establish a glass-house at Saint-Germain-en-Laye in 1551, and found its products 'of the same beauty and excellence as those that used to be imported from Venice'. It is perhaps worth noting that while on the whole the Altarist immigrants were far more liberal-minded than the Venetian glass-makers, they did not teach their craft to French workpeople during the sixteenth century. That came later and gradually, largely, as has already been noted, because many of them became legally absorbed into the population.

Of all this output of what must be considered fine as compared to ordinary glass, very little remains. Barrelet illustrates thirteen out of a possible twenty which can be classified as sixteenth-century Italo-French, and adds a warning that most of them could have been made at Venice, which was accustomed to decorate glasses to order. The same difficulty occurs in many cases with Bohemian, Silesian, Hall-in-Tyrol and Netherlandish glasses, all hopefully ascribed to this or that place of origin, but not necessarily anything more than examples of Venetian enterprise. There were however purely French houses which, even in the sixteenth century, claimed to be able to produce 'white' or 'fine' glass. Volcyr, for instance, wrote in 1530 of the manufacture in Lorraine of 'several kinds of fine glass resembling crystal'. He speaks also of a crucifix: 'A great glass cross, the thickness of a man's thigh, so richly decorated in colour that one was blinded by its beauty and splendour.'

Montpellier, to judge by a few inventories, for nothing of the sort has survived, had a reputation for enamelled glass. The inventory of the Prince de Condé in 1588 records 'three enamelled glass vases, *façon de Montpellier*'; in 1589 there is the inventory of Catherine de Médicis – 'two little vases of painted glass of Montpellier'. In addition to useful wares of all kinds there is evidence of a whole world of fantasy, for Rabelais speaks in 1546 of *'cent sortes de voyrres à pied, et voyrres à cheval . . . et telle semblable artillerie bachique* (a hundred types of glass in the form of foot soldiers and cavalry . . . and similar bacchic artillery').

With the seventeenth century the industry, as elsewhere, became more and more subject to regulation – and, as is often the way, less and less amenable to it. Communications were poor, forests widespread, the country enormous compared, say, to England, the State not yet fully in control of its grandees. The earlier grants of nobility, with all that implied in entrenched privilege, were the cause of endless disputes, and towards the close of the sixteenth century attempts were made to confine these privileges to glass-makers who could prove a noble ancestry. In 1603 Henry IV granted letters patent to the glass-makers of the Argonne, giving them freedom to manufacture and trade, but only if they were of noble descent. With one hand the State did what it could to reduce the number of non-taxpayers, with the other it conferred privileges upon certain individuals, both French and Italian, provided they could produce glass '*à la façon de Venise*'. As in England, this was the age of the monopoly system in France, by which a powerful individual would be given sole rights for a period of years; such men might be courtiers or enterprising speculators who knew nothing about glass-making but a great deal about finance and its methods of jungle warfare. Many small enterprises, however, carried on more or less outside the law, thanks to the help of individual landowners. It was not until the eighteenth century that the necessity to conserve forests induced the State to control the industry in earnest.

By the seventeenth century there were four main centres making fine glass, each protected by a monopoly, two of them directed by Italians (Nevers and Nantes), two by French owners employing Italians (Paris and Rouen).

The Loire Valley Monopoly

The founders, each of them from Altare, were the brothers Saroldo (Sarode) and Orazio Ponti. Their glass-house passed to G. Castellano (Castellan) after 1647 and he obtained a thirty-year concession in 1661 from the Crown, on the recommendation of Cardinal Mazarin; there were Castellans still in command in the eighteenth century, succeeded by members of yet another Altare family, the Borniolo, by now Borniol. Castellan senior shared his concession with his no less famous nephew Bernardo Perotto, better known to the French-speaking world as Bernard Perrot, who established a glass-house at Orléans in 1662. He was a man of many parts, credited with the invention of a substance which could be called porcelain – it was opaque-white or milk-glass – and certainly with a new method of making mirrors, a subject which has no place in this book; his invention was of sufficient importance for the Royal Factory management to register alarm. Perrot had to give way in return for the totally inadequate pension of 500 *livres* per annum.

The Paris Region Monopoly

This was built up by Jean Maréchal who, with the help of a *valet de chambre* of King Henri IV, secured in 1606 the exclusive right to manufacture and sell in Paris and the surrounding countryside for thirty leagues *façon de Venise* glass; he soon added rights over common glass. Among his victims was Antoine de Clerissy, a member of a family which made ceramic history; this was in 1641 and by then Maréchal had acquired the reputation of an ogre. He died in 1650, but in spite of the father's unpopularity the monopoly was renewed in favour of his son; it lasted until 1665, when Colbert authorized other glass-makers to sell their wares in Paris.

The Normandy Monopoly

This was set up in 1605 to make crystals, enamels, mirrors, *façon de Venise*, within the bounds of the local Parlement de Normandie. The first holder was François Garsonnet, a Frenchman from Aix-en-Provence. He established himself in Rouen with Italian workpeople, but after fourteen years sold out to the brothers D'Azémar, glassmakers from Languedoc, who have already been mentioned in this account and who had to ward off incessant attacks from long-established competitors, all anxious to make *façon de Venise* glass. The Rouen factory can claim that it was the first in France, perhaps even the first in Europe, to use coal satisfactorily instead of wood – no small achievement in an age of experiment with limited resources. The two brothers died and the business passed to the widow of one of them and her ten children. As elsewhere, the monopoly system was being gradually eroded and by 1665 the Rouen glass-house had to deal with competitors – and did so with considerable success for another hundred and five years.

Brittany

Its centre was Nantes, where Altarists set up a glass-house late in the sixteenth century and met with great success during the seventeenth.

The names are very much the same as at Nevers – Borniolo, Saroldo, Buzzone, for instance – and a certain Jean Ferro, who was knowledgeable in both glass and pottery and was evidently a man of exceptional ability and drive. He was responsible for at least four glass-houses in the region, in addition to pot-houses for the production of '*vesselle blanche*', i.e. the local faience. The district, considered as a glass-making centre, was more or less an Italian colony, and unlike the other three was not protected by a monopoly.

Glass-workers, particularly Italians – first the men from Altare, who were definitely encouraged by their guild, and then the Venetians who managed to escape from their cramped and cramping native island of Murano – were a wandering lot, and the industry – not merely in France – owes them a great deal. Quite apart from the four chief centres mentioned above, it is surprising how far afield in France their skill and enterprise took them. The same names occur again and again in widely scattered places both in France and the Netherlands. They staffed the various glass-houses of the Bonhomme family, whose headquarters were at Liège and who owned the factory at Verdun. The Saroldo at one time or another are heard of at Paris, Orléans, Rouen, Caen, Angers, Poitiers, Bordeaux, Toulouse, Lyons, Marseilles, Fontainebleau and in La Vendée. The Borniolo, in addition to working for monopolists, were to be found in Provence (1616), in the Drôme (1650), in l'Isère (1620), at Vienna (1680), in the Haute-Marne (1674). A similar story can be told of various members of the families of Mazzolao, Ferro and Buzzone.

In 1665 the king, on the advice of Colbert, left the industry to its own devices, with the exception of the manufacture of mirrors; this remained under Government control and, after several false starts, was from 1693 concentrated in what is now the great plant at Saint-Gobain. Thanks to Louis XIV it became the fashion to use mirrors for decoration, the most illustrious monument to that slice of social history being the Galerie des Glaces at Versailles.

By about 1600 Nevers was already famous for little enamelled figures, both men and animals, and became so well known for this speciality that, though such things were in fact made elsewhere, anything of the sort is inevitably credited to the town. The men appear to have worked there under peculiarly miserable conditions, if one can believe the account given by one traveller: 'If you were to see the dark, stifling, smoky, unhealthy dungeons where the enamellers have no light, day or night, except their lamps, you would be sorry for men condemned by necessity to such deadly work. These poor people, for the most part in poor health, are short-lived.' Other travellers speak of their importunate salesmanship, how they 'thrust their work upon you' in the inns of the Grand-Rue de Nevers 'and you accept it without being able to defend yourself'. However, a few became people of importance, patronized by the king and queen, the nobility and the municipality to manufacture presents for illustrious guests, though nothing of the sort which can be confidently ascribed to the sixteenth or the seventeenth century seems to have survived. One has to rely solely on documents.

Thus the *Journal d'Héroard* in 1605 tells how Louis XIII as a child played with 'little glass dogs and other animals made at Nevers'. The town archives record that when Louis XIII came to Nevers in 1622 he was presented with 'a work in enamel representing the victory His Majesty had gained over the rebels of the pretended reformed religion of the Isle of Ré – and also a *châsse*'. Another entry refers to a gift of chains and pendant ear-rings made by the town in 1625 to M. de Nevers while Mademoiselle de Nevers received chains, ear-rings and figures of Our Lady and of St Louis. There is also mention of a payment in 1629 for a similar gift to the Princess Marie. Such small objects were evidently very much *à la mode* for a long time, for chains and ear-rings as well as little cupids are mentioned by Jean Grillet, an enameller at Essones, in 1647, and in 1661 the *Journal de France et d'Italie* speaks of ear-rings from Nevers, together with rings and other jewellery. In 1691 and 1692 we learn of artificial eyes made by Hubin and Le Quin; we also learn that Hubin had been well known since 1673 for his barometers and thermometers, the latter the best until the time of Réaumur. Meanwhile a certain Roault specialized in all kinds of human figures, and the royal inventory for 1696 (*L'Inventaire du mobilier de la couronne*) lists nine market-stalls with little figures. Finally a book by de Blancourt, published in

1697, records 'diverse human figures, animals, birds and other curiosities'. The tradition lasted long and included Nativity scenes of a decidedly mawkish character and such witty little conceits as the two illustrated here: the mounted Henri IV by Charles-François Hazard (1758–1812) and the delicious Judgement of Paris by Haly, which can be dated to about the 1770s (figures 96 and 97); but it must be confessed that the majority of the Nevers groups which have managed to survive two centuries, whether religious or secular, are sadly lacking in charm by comparison.

Nevers became so famous as the centre for these small glass objects that it acquired the nickname of 'Little Murano', but the work was also carried out at other places from Rouen to Marseilles. Literary sources of various kinds list the following subjects: men, women, acrobats, musicians, grotesques, devotional figures, false gods, cupids, Christs, bouquets, flowers, butterflies, swans which swim in water, dogs, birds, imitation pearls, bracelets, purses and much else besides. Among the survivors are a cheerful set of the 'Four Seasons' in the museum at Nevers, various shepherds and shepherdesses with their sheep, while convents often ordered crèches, grottoes, deserts and other devotional compositions. One man in Paris, Jacques Raux, advertised in 1745 his 'little houses in which are pretty rooms'. One of these is in the Cluny Museum; it is a representation of a scene from the Italian Comedy, and on it is a ticket in which Raux tells the world that he makes all kinds of 'playful figures' (I think that in this connection that is the best translation for his word *grotesque*) 'to furnish cabinets and chimney pieces, beautiful pearl necklaces, earrings etc. He has also a cabinet filled with all kinds of curiosities and jewels and every year he invents novelties.' The fashion lasted until well into the nineteenth century.

This seems a convenient place in which to mention a development of glass technique which led to an interesting use for this magical material. The honoured name of Réaumur happened to occur on page 60 in connection with thermometers. In 1713, in an address to the Academy of Sciences, he looked forward to the day when it would be possible to manufacture a glass thread as thin and as flexible as that of a spider; in that case, he suggested, glass could be classed as a textile. No one took any interest in the idea at the time, but mixtures of silk and glass, imitating rich brocades, were exhibits at the exhibition of 1839. These so-called glass tissues were used chiefly for ecclesiastical vestments, and one of them covered the coffin of Napoleon when his body was brought back from St Helena for reburial in the Invalides. Réaumur has also been credited with the invention of white opaque glass, but this is a complete misunderstanding of his experiments at making porcelain. He began his researches in 1717, informing the Academy of Sciences of the results in 1727, 1729 and 1739, and also in a notebook which is appropriately preserved at Sèvres; but these experiments appear to have consisted of placing glass bottles in a crucible with a mixture of fine sand and gypsum. The result was of course not porcelain but an opaque glass; as opaque glass had been made in Venice from the fifteenth century onwards by other means this was no discovery, and his experiments in this field led to nothing.

Réaumur was not the only pure scientist eager to fathom the mysteries of the marvellous and mysterious substance which had so astonished Europe when it began to come over in quantity from the Far East during the seventeenth century; it was no doubt pure chance that decreed that the first true porcelain in the West should have been made at Meissen in Saxony by the obscure, persecuted and ultimately alcoholic Böttger.

In France the two successful and rival pioneers in the production of *porcelaine de verre*, or opaque glass ('milk glass', German *Milchglas*, Italian *lattimo*), imitating porcelain, were Bernard Perotto and Mazzolao (Perrot and Massolay, the latter Sieur de la Motte). The evidence seems conclusive. In *Le Livre Commode des addresses à Paris* in 1691 one reads the following: 'M. Perrot, Master of the Glass-makers' Guild at Orléans (*Maître de la Verrerie d'Orléans*) has discovered the secret of imitating Agate and Porcelain with Glass and Enamels.' And further on we read: 'It is reported that M. de la Motte whose fine work in enamels and glass in the manner of agate and porcelain was seen a few years ago at the Fair, intends to open an establishment in Paris.' This refers to Nicolas Massolay, son of Paul, who had been Perrot's chief competitor. In 1686 he had obtained an exclusive privilege, in spite of the opposition of Perrot, to manu-facture 'porcelains imitating those of China and agates imitating nature'. Perrot was joined in his opposition by Louis Pothenat, sieur de Saint-Estienne, a Rouen faience manufacturer. Massolay there-upon issued a challenge: that the two rivals should each, within two months, make a porcelain vase to be painted as the Court decided with a battle or a siege, an equestrian portrait of the King, or some such historical event – and, as to an agate vase, whatever kind of agate the Court chose. History is silent as to whether this test was ever carried out.

No glass that can be attributed to Massolay is known. There are a few which are, with some confidence, thought to be by Perrot, who was known for his mouldings and for the use of a translucid red colour.

The Eighteenth Century

Within the first twenty-five years of the eighteenth century the danger of deforestation, already recognized a hundred years before, was becoming serious. The Government at last took steps to enforce some sort of discipline, and many glass-houses opened up in places such as the neighbourhood of Caen, which could be served easily by English coal. The ancient fashion of encasing wine bottles in wicker was abandoned in favour of the English-type dark glass, while, in the upper ranges of the trade, the taste for *façon de Venise* glasses began to alter, thanks to the competition of crystal from Bohemia and, to a lesser degree, to that of English glass-of-lead. For a few years there was even a preference, in polite circles, for rough forest glass: 'In France now,' writes Savary des Brûlons, who died in 1716, 'one uses only forest glasses and crystal glasses are no longer in fashion: gour-mets are persuaded that wine is more delicate and delicious in simple forest glass; one hardly knows any more what are Venetian glasses.'

But as the years passed even the glass-makers of Murano were driven to imitate the moulded and engraved crystal of Bohemia so that (although this is an overstatement) there must have been occa-sions when the Venetians themselves were tempted to forget the age-old tradition and spectacular successes of their own craft. The result of all this is that he is a bold man who would venture, hand on heart, to assert definitely that at least half the surviving fine glasses were assuredly French and were not importations from Venice or Bohemia or elsewhere; in any case, so much of the work was carried out by immigrants or natives taught by immigrants that the question of origin seems not only irrelevant but also impertinent. We can say perhaps that the influence of Italian glass-workers on the slowly developing French industry was even more marked, and certainly as beneficial, as was the influence of Huguenot silversmiths and weavers in England. Apart from glass-houses all over France that specialized in the production of bottles which, at the beginning of the century, were onion-shaped with a fairly long neck, more like what the modern world would call a decanter, there were the many which made *façon de Venise* glass, others *façon de Bohème* glass and yet others *façon d'Angleterre* glass. Confusion could scarcely be worse confounded.

Of the first of these three categories the most celebrated were those of Nevers, of Orléans, of Chaillot and of Bayel; the last three of them petitioned in 1727 for an increase in the tax on imports from Venice. At Nevers the glass-house was directed first, between 1685 and 1721, by Michel Castellan, then by his widow and his nephew Bernard de Bormiol. The latter acquired the business for himself in 1726; later it was handed on to his widow, who kept it in operation herself until just before the Revolution of 1789. An interesting sidelight on the origin of these Nevers glass-makers is provided by the name of their headquarters, which in 1778 was still known as the Little Murano of Venice. At Orléans the glass-house of Bernard Perrot was taken over, after his death in 1709, by his relatives; with a privilege for twenty years in their pockets, they founded another glass-house at Fay-aux-Loges, which was bought by new owners in 1738 and thereafter made only bottles.

The glass-house at Chaillot, founded by Nicolas Massolao, obtained a fresh twenty-year privilege in 1706 to make all kinds of crystal glass; the claim was made for it in 1713 that it manufactured 'goblets of a new sort of crystal' which was fire-resisting – a claim which was

1 The Portland Vase. Cut cameo fashion, opaque white on blue, height 9⅝ ins, late 1st century BC or 1st century AD

2 The Lycurgus Cup. Opaque green but wine-coloured when viewed by transmitted light, height $6\frac{1}{2}$ ins, 4th century AD

3 Roman glass plaque, cobalt blue, height $7\frac{1}{6}$ ins, 1st century AD

4 Flask of greenish glass, height $6\frac{1}{8}$ ins, late 2nd century AD, from Cyprus

5 Handled flagon, bluish-green, rim outsplayed and folded up and in, height $11\frac{1}{4}$ ins, third quarter 1st century AD, found at Barnwell, Cambridgeshire

6 Wine-coloured jar with opaque white masks and white stripes on the handles, rim folded down, up and in, concave neck, height $9\frac{3}{4}$ ins, 1st century AD, found in Campania, Italy

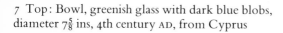

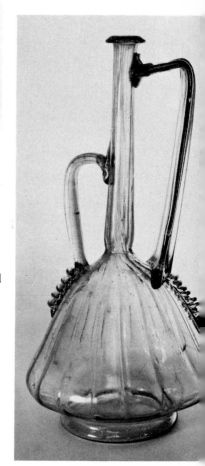

8 Bluish-green bottle, rim folded outwards, upwards and inwards, height $7\frac{7}{8}$ ins, 1st or 2nd century AD, found at Faversham, Kent

7 Top: Bowl, greenish glass with dark blue blobs, diameter $7\frac{5}{8}$ ins, 4th century AD, from Cyprus

9 Above: Ribbed bowl, bluish-green, rim folded out and down, diameter $7\frac{1}{2}$ ins, 3rd century AD, found at Faversham, Kent

10 Right: Slender flagon, olive green, rim outsplayed and folded up and in, height $9\frac{1}{8}$ ins, late 1st or early 2nd century AD, from Bayford, Kent

11 Bluish-green flagon, four pinches on rim to strengthen handle, height $7\frac{7}{8}$ ins, late 2nd or early 3rd century AD, from Bayford, Kent

12 Greenish-colourless jug, height $9\frac{7}{8}$ ins, 4th century AD, from Andernach, Germany

13 Buff colourless bowl, facet-cut, diameter $5\frac{5}{8}$ ins, 2nd century AD, from a grave at Leuna-Merseburg, Germany

14 Claw beaker, green glass, height $7\frac{1}{2}$ ins, *c.* 600 AD, found at Castle Eden, Co. Durham

15 Standing cup and cover, colourless glass, gilt ribs, above them blue and white thread, red dots, etc., height $16\frac{5}{8}$ ins, second half 15th century

16 Goblet and cover, clear colourless glass with enamelled and gilt decoration, height 18 ins, late 15th century

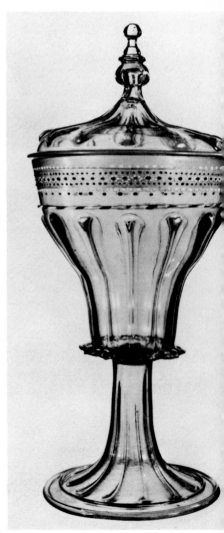

17 Enamelled bowl, height 6½ ins, 15th century

18 Standing cup, sapphire blue, height 6½ ins, mid 15th century

19 Emerald green goblet, ornamented with portrait medallions, young man and auburn haired girl supported by cupid, height 8⅝ ins, second half 15th century

20 Plate, opaque glass painted
in red, San Giorgio Maggiore,
height 8⅞ ins, 1741

21 Two-handled vase, opaque
white, 17th century

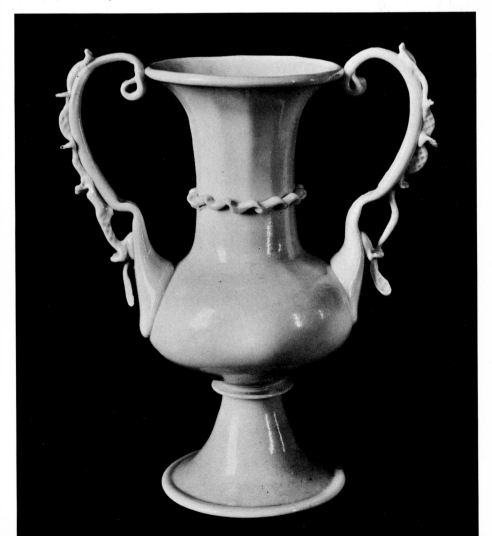

22 Covered beaker, opaque white, painted with rural scene, early 18th century

23 Bottle, opaque white, coat of arms on neck, enamelled, inscription on base 'Murano Miotti', height $9\frac{3}{8}$ ins, 1747

24 Tazza, colourless glass, diamond-point engraving, chain motif in centre in blue, diameter $10\frac{5}{8}$ ins, early 17th century, perhaps Spanish

25 Goblet, colourless glass, latticino, late
16th century, perhaps S. Netherlands

26 Three glasses: *left* goblet, blue, white,
red and gold, height 7½ ins, late 15th
century; *centre* goblet, white, blue and
gold, height 6½ ins, early 16th century;
right covered cup, diamond-point
engraving, early 16th century

27 Gadrooned bowl with blue threads, hollow spreading foot, dark blue border, height $10\frac{7}{8}$ ins, mid 15th century

28 Nef (ship), clear, turquoise and green glass, height 15 ins, 16th century

29 Goblet, colourless glass with three masqueraders, height $7\frac{1}{2}$ ins, late 16th century

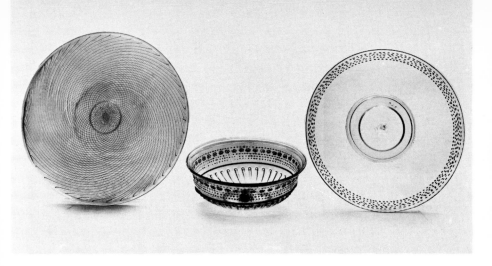

30 *Left* tazza, latticino spiral motif radiating from a central boss, diameter 10½ ins, *c.* 1600; *centre* bowl, enamelled in pale blue, white and gold with floral ornaments, ribbed moulded base, diameter 7¼ ins, 16th century; *right* tazza, blue and red dots, diameter 9⅜ ins, 16th century

31 Bottle, moulded with band of two lions and two double-headed eagles, swirling bands of latticino, height 7¼ ins, 17th century

32 Vase, enamelled in the Venetian manner, transparent uncoloured glass, height 10¾ ins, 16th century, Barcelona

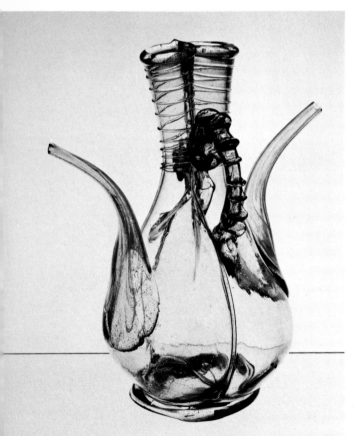

33 Vase, transparent green glass, threading and pincered decoration with eight tubular handles, height $7\frac{3}{4}$ ins, 16th century, probably Almeria Province

34 Vase, transparent smoky yellow glass, threading and pincered decoration, height 7 ins, 17th century, Granada Province

35 Double cruet, green glass with internal partition, trailed threading and pincered cresting on single handle, height $6\frac{5}{8}$ ins, 18th century, probably Granada Province

36 Vase, transparent green glass with threading and pincered decoration, height 6¾ ins, 18th century, Granada Province

37 Botijo, transparent yellow green glass with threading, trailed chain and pincered decoration, height 8¼ ins, 17th century, Granada Province

38 *Left* vase, Venetian style, yellowish glass, opaque-white combed decoration, height 6⅛ ins, 16th or 17th century, Barcelona; *centre* small jug, façon de Venise, opaque-white strands, blue handle, height 5⅛ ins, early 17th century, probably Barcelona; *right* biberon, opaque-white tape and twisted latticino, façon de Venise, 17th or 18th century, perhaps Spanish

39 Vase, transparent blue-green glass, overlaid with dark brown, brown handles and threading, height 5⅝ in, 17th or 18th century, Granada Province

40 Oil lamp, transparent blue-green glass, height 5⅛ ins, 17th or 18th century, Granada Province

41 Jug, pale straw-coloured glass, frosted, tooled handle, height 7½ ins, late 16th or early 17th century, Catalonia

42 *Left* vase, green glass streaked with brown diagonal ribbing, height 8 1/16 in, 18th century, probably Recuenco; *right* vase, uncoloured glass with diagonal ribbing, height 7⅞ ins, 18th century, probably Recuenco

43 Covered jar, crystal glass, engraved and fire gilt, faceted knob, height 20 ins, 1775–85, La Granja de San Ildefonso

44 Tray, crystal glass blown in the mould, engraved and fire gilt, 6¼ ins, wide, 1775–85, La Granja de San Ildefonso

45 Decanter, crystal glass blown in a fluted mould and enamelled, height 12½ ins, 1775–85, La Granja de San Ildefonso

46 Cruet (canadella), transparent straw-tinted glass, opaque-white combing, finial, vermicular collar, lip and foot plain, height 6 ins, late 16th century, Catalonia

47 Wine jug, blue-green glass, swan neck strap handle, the body decorated with ribs, spiral trail around the four lips, mid 18th century

48 Vase, two-handled, 16th or 17th century, Andalusia or possibly Castile

49 Jug, opaque white with bands of clear glass in between, silver-gilt mount, London 1548–9, height 6¼ ins, first half 16th century

50 Tazza, colourless glass, gilt prunts, height 6¼ ins, second half 16th century, S. Netherlands probably Antwerp

51 'Ice' glass, three lion masks, height 7⅞ ins, second half 16th century, S. Netherlands, probably Antwerp

52 Goblet, façon de Venise, white spiral decoration, height 11 ins, 17th century

53 Beaker, swirling opaque-white threads, façon de Venise, height 5¼ ins

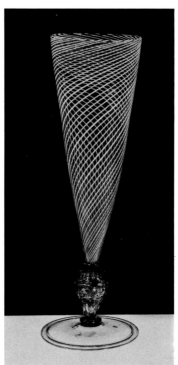

54 Wine glass, façon de Venise, diamond-point inscription, funnel bowl, height 6½ ins, 17th century

55 *Left* glass, diamond engraved, façon de Venise, yellow, orange and white convoluted stem, pincered blue wings, height 7⅝ ins, second half 17th century, perhaps Netherlands; *centre* façon de Venise, diamond engraved, winged and pincered stem with blue scrolls, height 6¼ ins, 17th century; *right* façon de Venise, knopped and pincered serpent stem, ornamented in blue, height 7⅝ ins, 17th century perhaps Liège

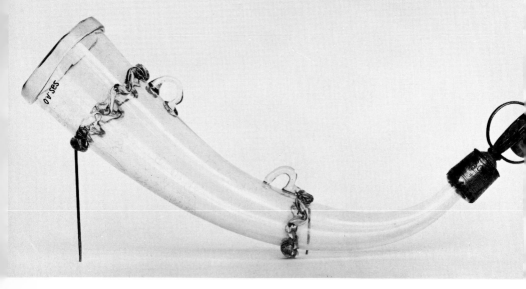

56 Drinking horn, diamond-point engraving '1595 21 Julet', colourless glass, length $12\frac{3}{8}$ ins, 16th century, probably S. Netherlands

57 Goblet, emerald green, gilt heraldic decoration, height $6\frac{5}{8}$ ins, c. 1600

58 Roemer, greenish glass, height 6⅛ ins, second half 17th century

59 Stangenglas, amber-green tint, height 8⅛ ins, 16th century S. Netherlands

60 Barrel-shaped glass, green glass with six finger grips, height 7⅘ ins, 17th century, Germany or Netherlands

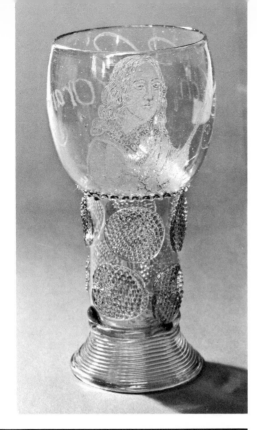

61 Roemer, greenish glass, diamond engraving, inscription in Dutch 'Still lives Orange', height 5¼ ins, second quarter 17th century

62 Roemer, diamond engraved, attributed to Anna Visscher, height 5¾ ins, c. 1650

63 Glass, diamond engraved by William Mooleyser, height 8 ins, c. 1685

64 Roemer, diamond engraved by G. V. Nes, Arms of William and of the seven united Provinces, height 9⅝ ins, *c.* 1687

65 Stangenglas, greenish glass, raspberry prunts, height 11⅜ ins, later 16th or early 17th century, S. Netherlands or Rhineland

66 Still life by Pieter Claes showing a beaker with prunts, signed and dated 1627

67 Still life by Jacob van Es showing two types of glasses, 17th century

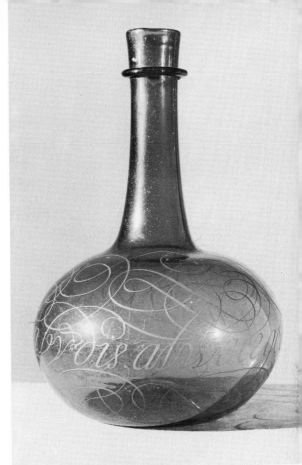

68 Goblet, faintly yellowish glass
engraved with diamond-point,
inscription, height 7¾ ins, c. 1660

69 Bottle, engraved by William van
Heemskerk, height 10⅜ ins, 1674

70 Goblet and cover, diamond
engraved, height 10 ins, c.1670

71 *Left:* Flute, colourless glass, diamond-point half length portrait of a young boy, coat of arms of House of Orange, inscribed 'Wilhelmus Prince d'Orange', height $15\frac{3}{4}$ ins, *c.* 1660

72 *Above:* Goblet, probably decorated 1657–8, Mary, Princess Royal of England, eldest daughter of Charles I and Henrietta of England, height $6\frac{3}{8}$ ins

73 Goblet, stipple
engraved by Wolff, The
Hague, height 7¼ ins,
1791, probably Newcastle

74 English glass, stipple
engraved by Wolff in
Holland, 1775–90,
height 7¼ ins

75 Armorial glass, stipple engraved by David Wolff, arms of William V of Orange, Newcastle glass, knopped stem, conical foot, height 6⅞ ins

76 Covered goblet, English glass of lead, engraved in Holland by Jacob Sang 1757, inscription, height 19½ ins

77 Beaker with three halberdiers

78 Goblet with the portrait of Pierre Tallon

79 Goblet with the arms of
Louis XII and Anne de Bretagne

80 Pommeraye goblet

81 Enamelled goblet, height 6⅜ ins, mid 16th century

82 Colourless glass height 8⅝ ins, 16th century

83 Vase, two-handled, colourless, height 14⅝ ins, early 17th century

84 Goblet on bell foot, façon de Venise, height 7¼ ins, 17th century

85 Beaker, octagonal sided, height 3 ins, 17th century

86 The Amiens Chalice. Height 6¼ ins, late 17th century

87 Moulded beaker from Orleans, by Bernard Perrot, mark – three fleurs de lys and a unicorn, the figures possibly intended for Louis XIV and Madame de Maintenon, height 3 ins, late 17th century

88 Moulded pot, colourless glass, diameter 3½ ins, 18th century

89 Three glasses from the Midi, 18th century: *left* Silesian stem; *centre* drawn trumpet bowl with with tear; *right* draw trumpet bowl; all three apparently façon d'Anglais

90 Three glasses, façon de Venise, height $5\frac{7}{8}$ ins, 18th century

91 Covered goblet, burette and jug, height $8\frac{5}{8}$ ins, 18th century

92 Lamp, clear glass, height 10⅝ ins, 18th century

93 Goblet, façon de Venise, late 16th or early 17th century, perhaps French

94 Sweetmeat vase and cover (*Drageoir*), mourning girl beside a broken column, monument inscribed 'Cigit L'Indifferent', height 6¼ ins, 18th century, Eastern France

95 Marbled glass pilgrim bottle, 18th century

96 Equestrian statue of Henri IV by Charles-François Hazard (1758–1812), 18th century, Nevers

97 The Judgement of Paris. Height 8¼ ins, 1777, Nevers

98 The Basket of Glasses.
Painting by Sebastien Stoskopf

99 Glass plaque engraved by
Casper Lehman, 1619 and 1620

102 Still life by Floris van Schooten, 17th century

100 *Opposite page:*
Covered goblet,
height 11 ins,
c. 1700, Silesia

101 *Above:*
Covered goblet,
engraved with SCR
beneath crown,
deep blue, height
$12\frac{1}{4}$ ins, 1701–05,
Potsdam

103 *Right:* Three
glasses, one 17th
century Roemer,
two Stangengläser
German

104 Beaker, ruby glass, height
4 ins, end of 17th century

105 Square flask, enamelled with
St Christopher carrying the Child
Jesus, 1697, Bohemia

106 Armorial Humpen,
enamelled in colours, 1683, Saxony

107 Two goblets, *c.* 1740; covered beaker, 1791

108 Jug, enamelled, dated 1573, Bohemia

109 Secular glass, enamelled hunt scene, clear glass tinted grey, height 26·2 cm, late 16th century, Bohemia

110 Ecclesiastical goblet, Zwischengoldglas, height $7\frac{1}{8}$ ins; wine glass, Zwischengoldglas, height $5\frac{1}{2}$ ins

111 Opposite page: Goblet, height $11\frac{1}{4}$ ins, Bohemia

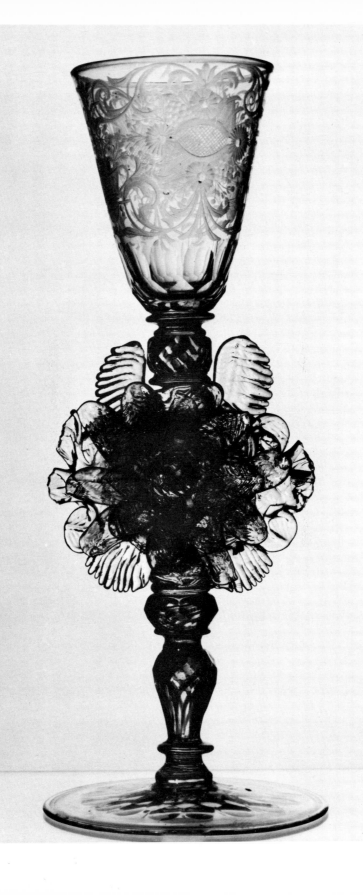

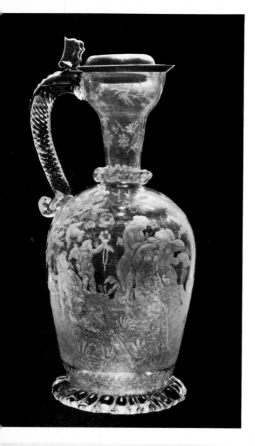

112 *Top:* Decanter jug, Ravenscroft, wheel–engraved with The Toilet of Venus in German or Low Countries workshop, *c.* 1676

113 *Left:* Beaker, dark blue enamelled in white, height 6¾ ins, 1599, Bohemia or S. Netherlands

114 *Above:* Covered goblet, Zwischen–goldglas, height 10½ ins, *c.* 1730, Bohemia

115 Two Stangengläser, Jacob Praun and his wife Clara, height 11¼ ins and 11 ins, probably, 1589, German (or Venice)

116 Beaker, blue, mauve and
green enamels, height 3⅝ ins, late
18th century, Bohemia

117 Goblet, colourless glass,
horsemen in grisaille, touches of
lilac, blue and green, background
bluish, height 8⅝ ins, c. 1740,
Bohemia

118 Ewer and basin, Schwarzlot, decoration
chinoiserie attributed to Ignatz Preissler, second
quarter of 18th century, Silesia or Bohemia

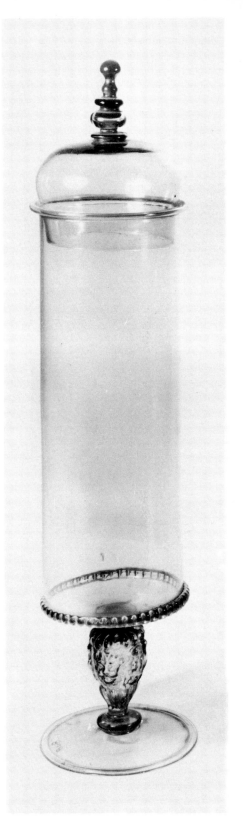

119 Top: Beaker or ice-pail, opaque white, height 9 ins, *c.* 1750–70, Bohemia

120 Above: Goblet, Hall-in-Tyrol, height 7⅜ ins, *c.* 1550

121 Right: Covered goblet, Hall-in-Tyrol, dark tinted glass, amethyst colour finial, height 15¼ ins, second half 16th century

122 Purple-glass, diamond-
point engraving, 9½ ins
diameter, 1613

123 Covered
goblet, green
glass, Nuremburg,
engraved by
Hermann
Schwinger, height
14¼ ins, late 17th
century

124 Passglas,
painted in bright
enamel colours,
height 10⅛ ins,
1719, German

125 Joke glass, height 11 ins, 17th century, German

126 Covered goblet,
colourless glass, applied
gilding in relief, height
14 ins, after 1733–4,
Dresden

127 Wine glass, enamelled
in relief by Johann Fredrick
Meyer, height $5\frac{1}{2}$ ins,
c. 1725, Saxon

128 *Left* Humpen,
enamelled with the Ages of
Man, height 7 ins, 1696,
Saxony; *right* Passglas,
enamelled with a playing
card, height $7\frac{3}{4}$ ins, Saxony

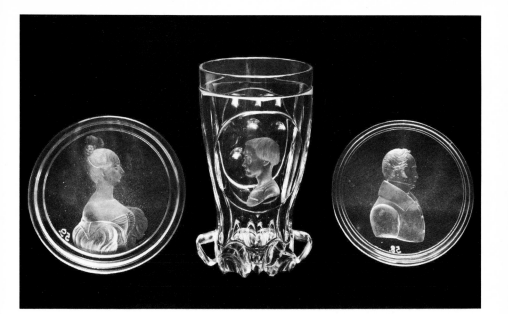

129 Three engraved portraits by Dominik Bimann, 1830s

130 Tumbler painted by G. S. Mohn, inscribed 'La Reconnaissance', 1812

131 Biedermeier cigar holder, manner of C. von Scheidt, height $6\frac{1}{4}$ ins

132 Beaker, Lithyalin, height $4\frac{1}{2}$ ins, *c.* 1830

133 Hyalith and Zwischengold Medaillon-pokal, height $7\frac{1}{8}$ ins

134 Service designed by Ludwig Lobmeyr, 1856

135 Service
designed by Joseph
Hoffman, 1920

136 Beaker,
enamelled on golden
wooden base,
designed by Lotte
Fink, 1925

137 *Left:* Crystal vase,
designed by Lehmden

138 *Above:* Presentation urn,
from the Federal President of
Austria, to the Shah of
Persia, height 14 ins, 1966

139 Crystal plate, cut by Franz Fritsche for
Lobmeyr, diameter 8¾ ins, 1870–85

140 Engraved jardinière, designer Ludvika
Smrckova, form dates from 1935, engraved 1945,
height 2⅞ ins

141 Sorbet glass, belonged to the Emp▮
Josephine, inscribed with letter J and cr◄
height 3⅜ ins

142 Tazza, wheel engraved, height $6\frac{1}{4}$ ins, 1862, Clichy-La-Garenne

143 Flower weight, unrecorded design, $3\frac{1}{8}$ ins, Baccarat

144 *Left* weight, lime yellow ground, 3 ins, St Louis; *centre* weight, faceted green with snake, $2\frac{7}{8}$ ins, St Louis; *right* weight, turquoise double over-lay, millefiori mushroom, $3\frac{3}{16}$ ins

145 *Opposite page:* The Oak Vase. Height 10 ins, 1859, by Emile Gallé at Nancy

146 A liqueur set, clear blue glass with gold and enamelled, height 9¾ ins, Emile Gallé

147 Vase, sweet peas, blue green and white, height 19¾ ins, Daum, influenced by Gallé

148 *Opposite page:* Gourd shaped vase, 'graal' glass, 1948, Edward Hald, Orrefors

149 Vase, engraved by Vicke Lindstrand, height 8¼ ins, about 1930, made at Orrefors

150 Bowl and bottle, 1948, by Edwin Öhrström, Orrefors

151 Vase, clear glass with engraved lines, *c.* 1946, designed by Tapio Wirkkala, Iitala Glass-works, Finland

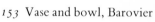

152 Vase, 1940, Venini

153 Vase and bowl, Barovier

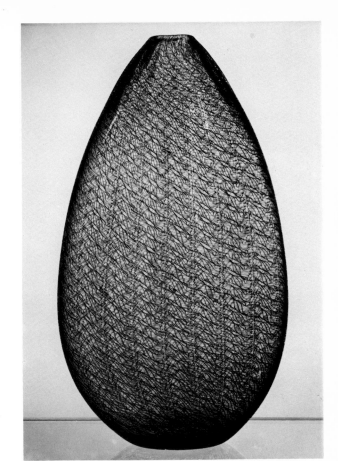

154 Clear glass with
threaded decoration,
c. 1951, by Archimede
Seguso

155 Two-handled vase,
rock crystal mounted with
enamelled gold, probably
Florentine, width $5\frac{1}{2}$ ins,
early 17th century

156 One of a pair
of Louis XIV rock
crystal table
candelabra, height
height 23 ins

157 Block of rock
crystal, 25 × 14 × 11
ins

certainly incorrect and which, it is thought, may have been made to improve the sale of opaque glass. The enterprise met with great difficulties and was eventually set up, in 1727, as the 'Sèvres Royal Glasshouse'. In 1750 the premises were given by Louis xv to Madame de Pompadour, who transferred the porcelain factory there from Vincennes three years later; it became the great Sèvres establishment, which still exists, while the glass-house was moved to Bas-Meudon to ensure that its fumes should not endanger the beauty of the Pompadour's newest, darling toy.

The Bayel glass-house, founded in 1679 by another Mazzolao to make crystal, was carried on after 1695 by his widow. From 1722 until the Revolution it belonged to the Villeprouvé family. This enterprise also had its difficulties, and in the 1720s had to shut down for a period because of foreign competition; but it reopened in 1727 and the *Journal historique sur les matières du temps* for 1728 informed the world that this glass-house was 'of all the greater benefit to the Kingdom in that it made a great many fine things for Spain, Portugal, Mexico, the Indies etc., based on the instructions and models sent by the Spanish and Portuguese merchants'. This is yet another hint as to the difficulty of identifying with certainty this or that glass which may happen to turn up on either side of the Atlantic.

Façon de Bohème and Façon D'Angleterre

While throughout the whole of the seventeenth century and until well into the second half of the eighteenth the many scattered glass-houses in France looked chiefly to Italy, neither the French nor even the Italians could wholly ignore developments elsewhere. By the end of the seventeenth century the quality of the engraved glass from Bohemia had gained it a substantial share of the better-class market, and though there were numerous French imitations there is ample evidence to prove that the Bohemian importations were preferred. The English flint-glass or glass-of-lead took many years to attract attention, and even then does not seem to have made any lasting impact compared to that from Bohemia.

The chief evidence for the condition of the French glass-houses during the second half of the eighteenth century is provided by that astonishing man of science Paul Bosc d'Antic (1726–84), who was both physician to the king and a practical glass technician. He was director of the enterprise at Saint-Gobain between 1755 and 1758 and in 1760 won the prize offered by the French Royal Academy for his thesis on the best means to improve the glass-houses of France – a report which was to become famous under the title of *Mémoire*. In this he notes how successful the English have been with their flint-glass, but he adds: 'They should not flatter themselves that their glass has reached perfection; it is not a good colour, yellowish or brownish, sometimes reddish when manganese is present in quantity.' In 1780, in one of several other reports, he adds that 'the English still furnish us with glass for optical purposes and both coloured and clear glass', but there is no mention of these productions in the advertisements of the dealers who regularly advertised Bohemian goblets. As early as 1725 an attempt was made to manufacture *façon d'Angleterre* glass at Chaillot but it came to nothing; it seems that the first place which could claim the honour was Chaumont-sur-Loire, near Blois, in 1772, with the help of an English glass-maker, Robert Scot Godefroi, who was invited in 1778 by the king's brother to set up a glass-house at Brunoy, near Paris. But Godefroi died and in 1779 a fresh permit was given to Joseph Koenig, a native of Bohemia, who said he had been employed for twenty-six years in one of the finest London houses and had experimented in Paris with both clear and coloured crystal. But Koenig's backer, a banker named Quévremont Delamotte, sacked him for drunkenness and incompetence; he seems to have ended up at Sèvres.

Meanwhile the royal establishment at Saint-Louis, which had been making glass *à la façon de Bohème* since about 1767, turned its attention to the English formula and, according to the judges appointed by the Academy of Science, the new French crystal was a perfect copy of the English metal. By 1788 seventy-six workpeople were employed at Saint-Louis in the manufacture of crystal, and sixty-one on window glass, out of a total of three hundred and sixty. Flint-glass was also imitated at Sèvres, but again without complete success. The opinion of Macquer in one of his reports for 1782 is quite definite:

'In truth in several French glass-houses clear glasses are made which are quite fine and to which one gives the name of crystal, but none of them have either the beauty or the weight of genuine crystal, i.e. that of England, and in general our French crystal does not enjoy a great reputation and is not, I think, much exported.'

In 1783 the glass-house for making crystal was established in the park at Saint-Cloud, near the Sèvres bridge, and the following year it obtained the patronage of Marie Antoinette under the resounding title of *Manufacture des Cristaux et Émaux de la Reine*. Workmen were brought from England 'because French workpeople are not able to deal with this substance which is wholly new to them'. Even so the enterprise met with no success, and was moved to Montcenis, near the coal deposits at Creusot, and there it survived throughout the Revolution. Other tentative enterprises met with even less success. There was Mayer Oppenheim, for instance, who came originally from Pressburg (Bratislava), worked for many years in Birmingham and in 1783 set up a little factory near Rouen; two years later it was employing eighteen skilled people, three of them English, three German, but we learn from a surviving letter that 'the objects were made without taste and were coarse'. Similar enterprises at Bordeaux and in Paris met with a similar fate. A few – a very few – glasses have survived which can be attributed to one or other of these ephemeral factories.

One can perhaps sum up the long and complicated story of glass manufacture in France up to the close of the eighteenth century by saying that, on the whole, its products display little originality as to form and are of rather poor quality material. Glass (apart from mirrors and stained-glass for windows, with which this account is not concerned) seems to have been the one substance and the one minor art that failed to engage the interest of the innumerable highly gifted Frenchmen who made so great a contribution to the amenities of civilization during the centuries discussed, however briefly, in this chapter.

French glass-making was destined to become important only in the nineteenth century and after. That story is part of the development of modern glass-making and will be dealt with, together with that of other nations, in a separate section.

The first six glasses illustrated are all from the sixteenth century. One cannot prove they are French, as Venice would sensibly and cheerfully decorate any glass to order and such glasses as these are inevitably in the Venetian tradition; who indeed at this time could escape so all-pervading an influence? At the same time their subjects and/or original owners were all French and there were numerous glass-workers in France, whether Venetians or Altarists, or even one or two Frenchmen, who were sufficiently skilled to make and decorate vessels of this quality.

The beaker of figure 77 is enamelled with three halberdiers dressed in the fashions of the brief reign of François II (1560), husband of Mary, Queen of Scots. This is in the Cluny Museum; with it, no less well-known, is the cup enamelled with the name of Pierre Tallon, Minister of Henri II, King of France between 1547 and 1559, and with portraits of himself and his wife (figure 78).

Figures 79 and 80 are equally famous and far more distinguished, the former decorated with the arms of Louis XII and of Anne de Bretagne. Louis reigned from 1498 till 1515, which fixes the date within narrow limits. The latter seems to me even finer, thanks partly to the diamond-point engraving of animals in a landscape round the bowl and the harmonious relationship between bowl, knopped stem and hollow foot. It bears the date 1578 and the arms of France (not visible in the illustration). It was made for Marthe Mansion de la Pommeraye, wife of a doctor in the province of Poitou, Gédéon Picard.

With figure 81 we are back in the mid-sixteenth century and among the somewhat naïve painters who exercised their skill in enamelling on the halberdier glass of figure 77 and the Pierre Tallon cup of figure 78. It is an odd little goblet from the mid-century, enamelled and gilt with a man, a woman and a white goat. The man is dressed in blue hose, red doublet, blue hat with a feather and is holding a spray of red flowers. The lady is holding a heart and says '*Mo Cveur Aves*' ('*Mon cœur à vous*'), while the man has a similar scroll before him which, in more orthodox spelling, announces '*Je suis à vous*'. Meanwhile the goat is trying to drink out of a narrow-necked vase. This is a play on the names of the two people represented: Jehan Bouceau and Antoinette Bouc (*bouc* means 'goat' and *eau*, 'water'). The last of these sixteenth-century glasses is a particularly graceful shape (figure 82); it has a hollow foot, an elaborate knop providing the whole of what in other types would be a stem, and a bowl of exceptional elegance.

With figure 83 we have reached the seventeenth century; it shows a double-handled classical covered vase with a ribbed lower portion, while the goblet in figure 84 owes a good deal to Venice, with its short stem and foot shaped as a bell. The octagonal-sided moulded beaker of figure 85 is clearly a good, sensible example of domestic glass which was no doubt produced by the thousand – the glass itself, one must add, is not of very good quality.

The double-handled vase of figure 86, in the British Museum, has been the subject of considerable argument in the past. It is of thick blue glass, with massive handles grooved to simulate rope and attached to the body in a most unusual manner. It was said to have been found near Amiens and purchased by the museum in 1865, when it was considered that it might date from as early as the fifth century AD; it has always been known as the 'Amiens Chalice'. The name survives, but the theory of a fifth-century origin has long been abandoned, partly because the 'chalice' has suffered from 'crizzling', a network of fine interior cracks that could eventually result in decomposition. 'Crizzling' is said not to have occurred in Roman glass, but it did occur in George Ravenscroft's experimental glass in England in the 1670s; therefore, according to one suggestion, the 'chalice' is English and possibly by Ravenscroft. But both the 'chalice' and a similar piece in the museum, which has lost its handles, have been analysed in the museum's research laboratory and have been shown to have an almost identical chemical make-up – a high potash content and a low lead content, whereas indisputable Ravenscroft glass so far analysed reveals a high proportion of lead.

There is, however, a third glass, sold at Sotheby's in 1947 and now in the Toledo Museum of Art, which has close affinities with the

'Amiens Chalice'; known as the 'Savoy Vase', it is blue, heavily 'crizzled' and has its two handles attached to neck and sides in the same unusual manner. This has always been described as one of Ravenscroft's experimental glasses of the mid-1670s and as being composed of 'lead metal', but so far no authority for its scientific analysis has been cited. On the other hand an analysis of two glass vessels considered to be from seventeenth-century France revealed results almost identical with those of the 'chalice' – potash about twelve per cent, lead between one and three per cent. The British Museum conclusion, in default of further evidence, is that the 'chalice' is French and late seventeenth-century, a conclusion re-inforced on grounds of style by comparison with certain faience vessels made at Nevers at this period. However tempting it may be to ascribe this fascinating rarity to England, someone must produce a group of indubitable Ravenscroft glasses with a similarly low lead content before the theory can be seriously considered.

The small vessels of figures 87 and 88 are good solid examples of moulded domestic glass from the late seventeenth century, the former ascribed to the glass-house of Bernard Perrot at Orléans (three fleur-de-lys and a unicorn) and decorated with two little figures; it has been suggested that they are intended to represent Louis XIV and Madame de Maintenon.

The three wine glasses of figure 89 are ascribed to a glass-house somewhere in the South of France and are pretty clearly in the English manner; all three should perhaps be dated to about 1730. The one on the left has the characteristic high-shouldered 'Silesian' stem which came into fashion in England after the Hanoverian succession in 1714, while the centre one has a drawn trumpet bowl made in one piece with the stem, which contains a characteristic air-bubble or tear.

None of this domestic table-glass is of any great quality, and the three wine-glasses of figure 90 clearly owe a great deal to Venice. The three pieces in figure 91, a covered goblet, a *burette* (for oil and vinegar) and a jug, are engaging, if decidedly clumsy, qualities which they share with the lace-maker's lamp of figure 92.

One cannot of course depend wholly upon photographs to form a judgement as to quality, but I think most readers will be able to see for themselves that the two pieces which follow (figures 93 and 94) are very much superior both in form and in material to the majority of the eighteenth-century glass which has preceded them. Figure 93, in the collection of the Victoria and Albert Museum, is a noble goblet with a hollow moulded knop and spiral *latticino* decoration, decidedly *façon de Venise*, but generally accepted as probably French from the late sixteenth or perhaps early seventeenth century. There is another goblet in the Victoria and Albert Museum that is perhaps a rather more likely candidate for French nationality, partly because the glass is dark in tone and so related to others which show the same characteristic imperfection and which, for one reason or another, can claim a French origin. It has been suggested that this graceful goblet may be from a glass-house started at Saint-Germain-en-Laye in 1551, with a privilege from Henri II, by the Altarist Theseo Mutio, but this seems no more than guesswork and other experts have attributed it to half a dozen Italian-operated glass-houses elsewhere. There is less doubt about the *drageoir* (covered glass for sweets) of figure 94; it is a fine, solid, no-nonsense receptacle from eastern France, decorated in enamels with a charming young woman leaning over a monument with a broken column on which is inscribed 'Here lies the indifferent [lover]' – she is a pensive girl, but one feels satisfied that quite soon she will be smiling again and will have found someone else who will not be 'indifferent'. This pretty, not too sentimental piece of non-sense is very French (compare it with a thousand odds and ends in porcelain and enamels) and very decidedly from the second half of the eighteenth century.

The pilgrim bottle in the next illustration (figure 95) is an example of marbled glass, with bright colours splashed on a light-blue ground, and is very attractive (to be compared with English Nailsea). It is in the Victoria and Albert Museum.

Finally there are the good-humoured little toys from Nevers which have already been referred to in the text. They are trivial enough, but are none the less highly accomplished, and deserve to be considered as in a class by themselves, to be discussed gaily and without portentousness. They are both to be seen in the Musée des Arts Décoratifs: figure 96, admittedly a minor masterpiece of its kind, is a mounted Henry IV, plumed hat and all, by Charles-François Hazard (1758–1812); and figure 97, 'The Judgement of Paris', dated 1777, shows the four figures of Paris and the three goddesses posed beneath a tree – a delicious nursery conception of the story.

It is almost a pity to return to the mundane world of useful, practical wine-glasses. The basket of glasses by the little-known Sébastien Stoskopf (figure 98), painted in Paris about 1640 and now in the Strasbourg Museum, provides convincing evidence of the type of glass in favour at the time and makes one realize how much has been lost. The painter deserves higher praise than that though. He was not anxious to make a record of facts for a curious posterity, but to put down in paint how light played marvellous tricks with glass. He has succeeded in painting a still-life of exceptional beauty.

6 Bohemia, Germany and Austria

The modern state of Czechoslovakia is very naturally eager to disclaim any close connection with the people next door. It is, however, impossible, amid the clash of empires and the squalid facts of national and dynastic rivalries, to ignore the map and pretend that each shifting political entity was an island insulated from its neighbours. The dictum that art knows no frontiers is a truth that is proved time and again throughout Europe's long, blood-stained history. It is no less true that one can generally, if often faintly, discern threads of a distinctive character running through parts of the whole wide tapestry which may justify the attribution of a particular section to a particular district. Perhaps, to change the metaphor, it is a flavour, rather than anything more definite; and to distinguish one wine from another requires experience and a sensitive palate.

To confess to a certain scepticism about some of the claims made by fervent nationalists on behalf of their respective countries is not to denigrate their contributions to the development of fine glass, but to emphasize the extreme difficulty of reaching definite conclusions. It has been necessary, for instance, in speaking of some of the glasses that appear to have been made in Spain or in France, to point out in many cases how unsure one is about the facts and how close many of the surviving glasses are to those produced elsewhere, whether in Italy, the Netherlands, or what is now Czechoslovakia, of which Bohemia forms a part. The difficulty of distinguishing between much of the seventeenth- and eighteenth-century glass of Bohemia, that of Venice and that of Bohemia's immediate neighbour on the other side of the Riesengebirge mountain range, Silesia, has puzzled everyone for generations. Silesia was not taken from the Habsburgs

73

until the middle of the eighteenth century, by Frederick the Great.

Glass-makers, on the whole, were a roving lot, partly of necessity, for they were constantly searching for fresh supplies of wood fuel; the forests were spread over vast areas, and differences in colour and in the quality of the material itself are known to occur in the production of a single glass-house. Moreover, documentary evidence is slight. There is yet further difficulty as we come closer to our own times, for several glass-houses in Bohemia owed their continued existence to the knowledge and enterprise of Louis Lobmeyr in Vienna. This part of the story will be dealt with in the chapter concerned with modern developments. It is mentioned at this point as an example of the danger of too rigid a classification on geographical lines. Would one be justified in that particular case in labelling the output of those Lobmeyr-controlled glass-houses as Austrian rather than Czechoslovakian? It was not merely a question of financial control, but of scientific management and an enlightened personal taste.

It is therefore with no surprise that, in modern scholarly catalogues, one finds exhibits frequently described as 'Dutch or German', 'German or Bohemian', 'probably Bohemian', 'possibly Netherlandish' and, no less vaguely, 'Central European'. With that warning always before one it is possible to navigate amid these numerous shoals with a good heart, knowing that it is unlikely that one will attain to absolute truth.

None the less, the fame of Bohemia as a glass-making centre is only second to that of Venice, is no less well-deserved and, on the whole, has outlasted that of its original mentor and rival, in spite of the political and social changes of four or five centuries, in spite too of the confusion inevitably caused by the fact that over an immense area – Hanover, Hesse, Brandenburg, Saxony, Bavaria, Bohemia, to mention merely half a dozen independent or nearly independent states – very similar styles were in fashion from time to time. In its early days the Bohemian industry produced, in addition to window glass, simple beakers in forest glass and little more. A few – a very few – glasses of quality have survived from the early fifteenth century; one of them, a beaker with applied prunts, is in the Museum of Industrial Art in Prague and was excavated in the town of Sezimovo Usti, in southern Bohemia, a place which was completely destroyed in 1421.

During the sixteenth century there were in Bohemia alone as many as thirty-four glass-houses, so that the Emperor Maximilian, alarmed by the depredations made on the forests, endeavoured to call a halt to expansion; but the great nobles, almost independent princelings paying attention to Vienna only when it suited them, took little notice – glass manufacture was profitable.

As elsewhere, in Murano itself, for instance, and in France, the industry enjoyed many privileges denied to ordinary trades; its members were exempt from the normal feudal obligations and, though more rarely, could be granted letters of nobility. Of several distinguished men thus ennobled the best known is Caspar Lehman, jeweller and lapidary, who worked at the court of the Emperor Rudolf II at Prague, first as a carver of rock-crystal and then as the initiator of engraving upon glass, for which Bohemia established so great and deserved a reputation. One beaker actually signed by him and dated has survived; it is an armorial beaker engraved with allegorical figures of *Nobilitas*, *Potestas* and *Liberalitas*, signed 'C. Lehman 1605'.

Rudolf II was eccentric and more than normally politically inept, shutting himself up in his palace with a mixed menagerie of animals, women, painters, sculptors, mathematicians and astronomers (among the latter Tycho Brahe and Kepler); but perhaps he was in fact of greater service to civilization than politically-minded historians give him credit for. One can at any rate argue that he was genuinely devoted to science and the arts and that the disasters of his reign and its cruelties were due more to deficiencies of character than to deliberate wickedness. The Victoria and Albert Museum has three rectangular panes of glass engraved by Lehman. One of them (figure 99) is engraved with the story of Perseus and Andromeda and, above that, with the crowned initials of the Elector Christian II of Saxony, who died in 1611, and of Hedwig, daughter of Frederick II, King of Denmark, whom he married in 1602. The other two panes are engraved with animals and trees and are dated 1619 and 1620. All of them are pure wheel engraving, unpolished and with no trace of the diamond-point engraving which was sometimes used in addition by Lehman's successors at Nuremberg. The Emperor had granted him a privilege for engraving upon rock-crystal and glass; this Lehman bequeathed at his death in 1622 to his pupil Georg Schwanhardt (1601–77), who then returned to his native city of Nuremberg. With his two sons and three daughters he seems to have been the chief personality in a whole school of engravers who made Nuremberg almost as famous for its engraving on glass, both wheel and diamond-point, as it had long been for its silver and silver-gilt. One of these artists, Johann Heel (1637–1709), was at once glass-engraver, silver-smith, engraver of prints and painter on faience; another, perhaps better known, was Herman Schwingler. But both here and elsewhere the mantle of Lehman had fallen upon many anonymous, humble people unknown to fame, working in widely separated areas.

Apart from Nuremberg three centres during the last half of the seventeenth century and the first half of the eighteenth produced work well above the ordinary. The first was the glass-house set up in Silesia under a privilege granted by Count Christoph Leopold von Schaffgotsch to Friedrich Winter for the engraving of glass in the manner of crystal. Winter built a mill driven by waterpower at Petersdorf in 1690–1 and there engraved certain goblets in the cameo-relief technique (*Hochschnitt*), which are as near the much admired rock-crystal as it is possible to get in glass (figure 100).

The second was a workshop set up in Berlin in 1687 by Martin Winter, brother of Friedrich, who had as his patron Friedrich Wilhelm, Elector of Brandenburg. This also produced *Hochschnitt* engraving (generally considered impossibly laborious work, at any rate for Europeans, without water-power) and the more usual intaglio (*Tiefschnitt*). Winter's pupil, and a better artist, was Gottfried Spiller, who was responsible for a covered goblet in the Victoria and Albert Museum, dating from about 1700. It has a charming design of children gathering grapes.

The third was the glass-house at Cassel, presided over by Franz Gondelach, whom most experts consider to be the greatest of the

German engravers; he was born in 1663 and was still *Hofglasschneider* ('court glass-cutter') at Cassel in 1716.

The high repute of Bohemian glass before the close of the seventeenth century – and Bohemia, it must again be noted, included Silesia until 1742 – was due not merely to the skill of its engravers who so exactly interpreted the rather showy, ostentatious taste of their day, but to the quality of the metal itself. While the English were developing their glass-of-lead, the Bohemians were perfecting what came to be known as 'Bohemian crystal' by adding limestone to the mixture; after many experiments this resulted in a glass of singular purity, well suited for deep engraving. By the close of the seventeenth century and the beginning of the eighteenth it was this glass that became the leader in world markets. Madame L.Uresová in her introduction to the Victoria and Albert Museum exhibition of Bohemian glass in 1965 sums up the position at this time in these words:

The absolute purity and high lustre of the glass material, the original designs and a rich profusion of decorative themes made every piece a unique *objet d'art*. Baluster goblets with ornamental cut stems, enhanced after the year 1700 with the further ornamentation of *aventurine* or ruby glass threads, had their conical bowls decorated with cut and polished facets. They were further decorated with portrait engravings of important contemporary personalities, cleverly framed in leaf and floral designs, strapwork, shells etc., distributed in profusion all over the surface. There were also views of town architecture, Biblical and allegorical scenes, genre or hunting scenes, coats of arms of the principal aristocratic families or ecclesiastics, set against a rich background of strapwork, acanthus foliage and scroll ornament. The same type of ornament was also used on faceted stemware, or bowls with cut and polished sides, perfume bottles, decanters and crystal glass barrels.

A little later – say about 1725 – the Czechs devised a new trick: double-walled glass enclosing etched gold or silver foil, often also stained in transparent colours and engraved (*Zwischengoldglas*). Perhaps, though, one should be cautious in speaking of devising new methods, but should instead write of rediscovering old ones, for there are fragments, probably of the twelfth century, which are decorated with engraved gold-leaf between two layers of glass, either from Egypt or Syria. After all, such a masterpiece as the Portland Vase in the British Museum is sufficient evidence of the uncanny skill of glass-makers in the world of Imperial Rome in the technique of cutting through a white opaque outer casing, leaving the inner layer to provide a dark background; the result is known as 'cameo glass'. It is a tribute to their accomplishments that a satisfactory replica of the vase was not made until John Northwood senior managed to produce one in 1876.

Among glass-makers and engravers (in addition to those already mentioned) whose names have not merely survived but who can be said to have played an important part in the development of their craft was the chemist Johann Kunckel, who had published the first edition of his *Ars Vetraria Experimentalis* in 1679, based upon the pioneer treatise of Antonio Neri (1612), which included many formulae for coloured glass. Neri himself had acquired much of his information from the glass-houses of Antwerp that had been founded by Venetians. Kunckel, however, was able to go further, either during or before 1679, by manufacturing a ruby glass by means of gold chloride, the first time that the invention of Andreas Cassius of Leyden was put to practical use. A very small proportion of gold (as little as one part in a hundred thousand) is needed to produce the ruby tint in glass. The 'purple of Cassius', as it was called, after its inventor, had of course wider uses; among other triumphs it revolutionized the enamel decoration on Chinese porcelain, making possible the opaque rose-pink which was destined to give its name to the eighteenth-century *famille rose*.

By 1689, when the second edition of his book was published, Kunckel was adding a proportion of lime to his formulae, no doubt learning from Bohemian practice. He was the director, from 1679, of the glass-house at Potsdam, which, like the engraving workshop of Michael Winter, was also under the protection of the Elector Friedrich Wilhelm; after the latter's death in 1688 his experimental glass-house was burnt down and he seems to have been manoeuvred out of his position – another victim, it would appear, of the rat-race.

However, he was too big a man to be ignored; he made a journey to Sweden in 1693, was soon afterwards ennobled as Kunckel von Löwenstern and died in 1703. But the Potsdam establishment which he had set on its feet continued to prosper; it was moved to Zechlin in 1736 and remained in operation under the aegis of the State until 1890. The imposing covered goblet of figure 101, from the British Museum, is of a deep blue metal engraved with 'S.C.R.' beneath a crown, framed by two large fronds of laurel (the letters stand for Queen Sophia Charlotte, sister of George 1 of England and wife of Frederick 1 of Prussia). It is from the Potsdam glass-house and can be dated with exactitude. The dukedom of Prussia was elevated into a kingdom in 1700, the Queen was crowned in 1701 and died in 1705.

There were two main types of drinking-glass that were more or less standard throughout the German-speaking, beer-drinking lands. One was the *Stangenglas* ('pole-glass') – a tall cylindrical beaker with a spreading foot. It was sometimes encircled by a notched spiral thread dividing it into equal parts; the guest would be expected to drink down to one of these divisions before passing it on and this variant was known as a *Passglas*. The other and far more familiar type was the *Roemer*, seen in dozens of seventeenth-century Dutch and Flemish still-life paintings, and for centuries the glass for Rhenish wine. The shape goes back at least to the fifteenth century: at first it was a conical beaker with small glass drops applied on the lower part, but this soon developed into the normal seventeenth-century pattern of bowl, wide, hollow stem impressed with a raspberry pattern of raised drops (which the English trade knows as 'prunts'), while the foot was formed by a continuous spiral thread (or in modern practice by a series of close-set raised rings).

It is remarkable how the *Roemer* has kept its popularity and even its traditional green colour in the modern world; it continued to be made with the greenish tinge of the old medieval forest glass long after methods of decolorizing were generally known. The shape can scarcely be described as elegant, but it is at once practical, cosy and comely and well deserves its universal appeal. Its interest for the painters was of course not a tribute to its quality; it happened to be a glass which was always at hand, as common an object as the fruit, cheese, pewter and other objects with which it is associated, and so it was not necessary to search for a model, an exceptional rarity. It also provided a challenge to any artist, who had to decide how to deal with the quality of light as reflected in it and in its contents. However, in this book we are not concerned with these high matters – merely to record the fact that seventeenth-century painters used these engaging glasses in their meticulously observed pictures more than any other. The still-life by Floris van Schooten illustrated in figure 102 was seen a few years ago at the Brod Gallery in London and is an admirable example.

The three glasses in figure 103 appeared in a dispersal at Sotheby's. In the centre is a green-tinted *Roemer*, on either side of it a *Stangenglas*.

Of the survivals of baroque magnificence from the late seventeenth century the covered goblet of figure 100, from the Beck Collection sold at Sotheby's, is as impressive as any with its deep-cut, swirling forms and air of lavish opulence, exactly epitomizing the ideals of an age which had little admiration for understatement or reticence; nothing better exemplifies the debt that the glass-makers owed to ancient tradition, to the tradition of the lapidary working on a lump of the much admired rock-crystal. This is the sort of goblet which, nearly a century earlier, in a slightly different style, Lehman might well have carved in rock-crystal for his master the Emperor Rudolf at Prague before attempting work upon glass. As it is it comes from the works owned by the Schaffgotsch family in Silesia, whom we have already mentioned. This is *Hochschnitt* or 'deep engraving'; its form is that of a cornucopia, the cover surmounted by a stylized bud knop, the whole covered in broad-leaved scrolling foliage and with a bird on each side. It may be a trifle flamboyant for modern taste, but once one can accept the conventions of its day it stands out as a masterpiece, not merely because of the skill of the engraver, but because of the balance and harmonious relationship between its various parts. This is where the art of the glass-maker can achieve such flexibility – he has devised a noble shape before the engraver has raised his hand to it.

The thick-walled goblets and covers, decorated with engravings and often fluted, are distinctively Bohemian, beginning in about the year 1680. Bohemian influence spread far and wide. Goblets of this character would be made to individual order – decorated perhaps with merchants' wagons or ships, views of towns, allegories of peace and war, occasionally as souvenirs; one example is a glass engraved with an equestrian portrait of the Emperor Leopold i and the Sultan Mustapha ii to commemorate a peace treaty with Turkey. A later glass engraved with the imperial two-headed eagle and allegorical figures of Bohemia and Silesia is a reminder of the loss of the latter province to Prussia in 1742.

Compared with the fluent, apparently effortless handling of the Schaffgotsch goblet, the beaker in ruby glass engraved cheerfully with naked *amorini* carrying swags of fruit and leading a goat appears rather clumsy, a criticism resulting from its down-to-earth shape rather than the quality of its engraving. This is also late seventeenth-century and from the glass-house at Potsdam (figure 104).

A more conventional type of German engraved goblet was engraved by S.Schwartz in 1719 at Nuremberg with a portrait of Prince Eugene on one side plus symbolic figures and an inscription, the bowl supported on the high-shouldered and fluted 'Silesian' stem which also became fashionable in England after the accession of George i in 1714.

Another method of decoration which was in favour everywhere over a lengthy period was, of course, painting in enamel colours, a fashion learnt from Venice; it was used particularly for beer-glasses called *Vilkums* ('welcome glasses'), which were specially ordered for welcoming important visitors and were generally ornamented with the coat of arms and escutcheons of the family. The oldest survivor of this comparatively large class of Bohemian glass is a beaker painted with the arms of the Koc of Dobos family, dated 1574, while other, less personal designs, were the eagle, symbol of the Empire, stylized portraits of the Emperor as Holy Roman Emperor attended by the seven imperial electors and illustrations from the Scriptures or popular moralities.

Some Bohemian glass-painting has a peasant naïvety about it which makes it particularly attractive, in striking contrast to the worldly sophistication of engraved glasses of the standard of the Schaffgotsch goblet. An eloquent example of this simple charm is the square flask of figure 105, enamelled in colours with St Christopher carrying the Child Jesus across the waters. It is dated 1697 and so was made within a year or two of the cornucopia *Hochschnitt* goblet.

Another decorative method in vogue in the seventeenth century for which the credit is given to Johann Schaper (1621–70) is *Schwarzlot*, enamel painting, mainly in black. Schaper, a *Hausmaler*, an independent decorator working at home and exercising his craft on both pottery and glass, is recorded at Nuremberg in 1655 after working at Ratisbon (Regensburg) and had many followers in both Germany and Bohemia. The glass in figure 106 is Saxon, is dated 1638, and is ornamented with two unidentified coats of arms. Each of them is typical of its time and of the rather coarse, uninspired heraldic painting provided to order by numerous glass-houses.

With figure 107 we are in eighteenth-century Bohemia; the two tall goblets on each side of the covered beaker are at once gay and dignified and decorated in *Zwischengoldglas*. Their date is about 1740 and each depicts a cheerful social occasion; presumably each would have been a special order. The one on the left shows a terrace on which two couples are conversing, while on the other side are a dolphin fountain and a gazebo. The glass on the right depicts a betrothal scene: a man presenting another man to a young woman, dogs, servants, refreshments and an inscription – 'Long Live the Engaged Couple'. The covered beaker in the centre is much later and can, from its subject, be dated accurately. It represents the balloon ascent which Lunardi made at Naples in 1791 in the presence of the king and the court, who are seen in the foreground; this is a light-hearted, good-humoured vessel, which appears to be of exceptional rarity, for it is carried out by means of coloured paper and straw between two walls of glass.

Let us return north to Bohemia: the jug of figure 108 is painted in enamels with a Crucifixion and formal plant scrolls and is dated 1573, while the secular glass of figure 109, also in enamel colours, is of roughly the same date and in any case not later than the closing years of the sixteenth century; it depicts a very lively little hunting-scene with four huntsmen, two rabbits, boars, a stag and a bear; the glass is clear with a greyish tint. The tall goblet in figure 111 dates from about 1700 and is a rare example from Prague; it was seen in London in 1965 at the Victoria and Albert Museum exhibition. The Bohemian glass-workers have paid tribute to earlier Venice fashions by a fantastically elaborate knop above the baluster stem and exhibited their own special skill as engravers on the bowl.

Of the two glasses in figure 110, the wine-glass on the left with the polygonal funnel bowl is in *Zwischengoldglas*, decorated with a stag-hunt; the goblet next to it, in the same technique, has a fox-hunt on the reverse, on the other side a coat of arms and a cardinal's hat.

The near impossibility of keeping these European glasses within rigid geographical boundaries is illustrated eloquently enough by the next three photographs. The two *Stangengläser* of figure 115 are probably German but possibly Venetian. They are painted with portraits of Jacob Praun holding two flowers and his wife Clara in a gold dress with a white muff and holding a single flower. The decanter jug of figure 112 is English. It is a very rare piece by George Ravenscroft of about 1676, but was wheel-engraved with the Toilet of Venus in some German or Low Countries workshop, well before eighteenth-century Newcastle glasses became popular among Dutch engravers because post-Ravenscroft English glass was so well adapted to their purpose. The early beaker of figure 113 – it is dated 1599 – is of dark blue glass, enamelled mostly in white, the design divided into three compartments, two with hounds, the third with a stag. It is attributed either to Bohemia or to the southern Netherlands. A beaker of ruby-glass from South Germany, in style, not so much of the design but of the calligraphy, points to Holland. Cupid floats on the water seated on his quiver while the reverse is inscribed *Amour Trouve Moyen* ('Love finds a way').

There is no doubt whatever about the five glasses which follow: they are all Bohemian. Figure 114 is an admirable example of *Zwischengoldglas*: it is a handsome covered goblet, with a continuous stag-hunting scene. The beaker of figure 116 is rather later; it dates from the second half of the eighteenth century and is painted in blue, mauve and green enamels. The goblet of figure 117, to be dated to about 1740, has a more elaborate decoration but is not so effective, the painter having fussed too much over details. The distant background is bluish, the figures executed in *grisaille* with touches of lilac, blue and green. The foot is painted with sprays of foliage. At the base of the bowl is a flattened bulb of bright orange, while the stem beneath is formed by a spirally ribbed bulb and a smaller faceted one; through each of these runs a ruby cord.

The ewer and basin of figure 118 is an altogether finer piece of work, its decoration neatly married to its shape; the artist – whoever he was – recognized the limitations imposed upon him by the material, for he has not treated a glass vessel as if it were merely a painter's canvas. The technique is that of *Schwarzlot* picked out in gold, the subject the gay chinoiseries in fashion during the first half of the eighteenth century. The decoration is attributed to Ignatz Preissler (b. 1676) who was working at Kronstadt in Bohemia in the service of Count Franz Karl Liebsteinsky von Kolowrat from 1729 to 1739.

The beaker (or ice-pail) of figure 119 is an example of opaque-white glass made in many places between 1750 and 1770 in imitation of porcelain; painters were frequently employed on both. The sides are enamelled with four scenes, each containing a man and a woman and illustrating the Four Elements.

An early glass-house at Hall-in-Tyrol enjoyed a brief period of fame and its output for a time was not without distinction, though, as in so many other cases, there is occasionally a difference of opinion as to whether some of the glasses generally attributed to it should not be placed to the credit of Venice. It was founded in 1534 and enjoyed its most prosperous years between about 1550 and 1570 under the direction of the Augsburg merchant Sebastian Hochstetter. In due course it came under the protection of the Archduke Ferdinand – here, as elsewhere, princely patronage was essential. The glass-house made colourless glass, but is better known now for its greens and blues, often diamond-engraved, sometimes enamelled and gilded; but the colours were unfired and therefore easily destroyed, a casual, hopeful practice which seems to have been a characteristic of the factory. Venetian influence is very marked, as is clear enough in the glass illustrated in figure 120, and there would appear to be, on balance, sufficient justification to attribute it to this enterprise at Hall. The tall covered goblet of figure 121 is more obviously inspired by northern conventions; it is an attractive glass, its stem formed as a hollow-blown lion mask and gadrooned knop, the metal dark-tinted and with an amethyst-coloured finial.

The tall covered goblet of figure 123 is a worthy representative of a large class of Nuremberg glasses of the late seventeenth century, in which the highly elaborate fashions in favour with the silversmiths of the period have been disciplined down to something more in keeping with the nature of glass, their effect depending largely upon colour contrasting with colourless knops in stems and finials. The goblet is green and is further distinguished by its wheel-engraving, a continuous wooded landscape with a ruined castle and a shepherd with his flock; the artist was Hermann Schwinger (1640–83), one of the many Nuremberg engravers who could trace their artistic descent from Caspar Lehman. Another notable engraver working until 1726 was Georg Friedrich Killinger; there is a goblet by him in the Victoria and Albert Museum decorated with a landscape.

One has to be a trifle vague about the splendid purple glass plate of figure 122 with its diamond-point floral engraving; it is dated 1613 and could have come from any one of half a dozen centres; needless to add, it is more than an ordinary rarity. Similarly, caution is necessary in trying to pin down the *Passglas* of figure 124 to a particular glass-house. It is dated 1719 and painted in bright enamel colours – a lively example of simple, nursery-style humour. So is the rather earlier joke glass of figure 125, dating from the late seventeenth century; when one wishes to drink from it one's finger must press on the appropriate aperture if disaster is to be avoided. One is on firm ground with the dignified covered goblet of figure 126 and the wine-glass of figure 127: both are from Saxony, the covered goblet not earlier than 1733. It is ornamented with applied gilding in relief and eight lines of inscription. On the cover is a boar-hunt and a stag-hunt; on the bowl the monogram 'A.R.3' appears in a cartouche beneath a crown, over which is the motto 'Vivat'. 'A.R.3' refers to Frederick Augustus, born 1696 and Elector of Saxony 1733. He was chosen King of Poland later in that year, was crowned at Cracow in 1734 and died in 1763. Figure 127 is inscribed '*Un Seul me suffit*', the enamelling ascribed to J.F.Meyer; on one side is a basket of fruit, on the other a landscape in which a cupid holds a garnet heart in his right hand. He has no left arm – an odd early eighteenth-century whimsy.

Finally, there are the two German glasses of figure 128. The first is a *Humpen* dated 1696 and enamelled with the Ages of Man, probably from some Saxon glass-house. The other, the *Passglas*, is dated 1723 and decorated with a playing-card. This is also Saxon. Each is a good and rare example of clumsy, attractive naïvety, very different from the sophisticated grace, both in form and decoration, of so much of the glass from other parts of Europe. They were both in a sale at Christie's.

7 The Nineteenth Century and After

With the Napoleonic Wars and the Industrial Revolution the art of glass, like the other arts, fell upon evil times; not, I hasten to add, from the technical point of view, for these years – the first half of the century – saw the beginnings of a vast expansion of the industry as new markets absorbed new production and as a new middle class demanded a share in what had hitherto been possible only for the few. Manufacturing know-how had brought this marvellous material within the reach of everyone and its widespread use, not only in people's homes but for industrial purposes, made it inevitable that, for a time, its value as a workaday metal would be appreciated far more than its inherent challenge to the artist's imagination.

It is a little difficult, none the less, to pin down the reasons for the changes of taste during the first fifty years of this century which culminated in the curious horrors in England of the Great Exhibition of 1851 – horrors which were not confined to England but were greatly admired all over Europe. We have seen something like this riot of kitsch in our own day, and have nothing to boast about; a nation which in the 1970s can tolerate painted plastic gnomes in its suburban gardens has no right to sneer at the niggling excesses of much Bohemian and other glass of the 1840s. Popular taste obeys its own laws and no one has yet been able to define them, which is not really surprising, because no one can produce a satisfactory definition of 'taste' – a neutral word which requires the addition of an adjective before it can make any impact.

In spite of the growing menace of mass-production, which brings immense benefits in the long run but which is liable to plunge a whole great industry into useful commercially profitable banalities to the neglect of imaginative enterprise, there were a few men in the earlier years of the century who had something original to contribute, the most interesting of them being Dominik Biemann or Bimann (1800–57), who is best known for his engraved miniature portraits. The three illustrated in figure 129, to be dated from dress and hair-style to the 1830s, are characteristic examples of Bimann's sensitive, rather dry manner, giving the impression that he was keeping a very tight hold over himself at every moment. These portraits in glass are a natural extension of the miniature painting in vogue at the time, with this difference: a painter can erase his mistakes, but a glass-engraver working on so small a scale cannot afford a slip.

Bimann, one among many engravers in the then Austro-Hungarian Empire who were only a step or two behind him, was born at Nový Svět and learnt his craft there at the local glass-works, the Harrach plant, the largest in Bohemia at this time; its three cutting shops, together with three other private shops, employed between them about a hundred cutters, fourteen engravers, ten stainers and gilders, three specialists in glass beads and products of wound glass, and one badge engraver. Like many others at this period, he found it profitable to visit the various spas, where there was a steady demand for portraits. He studied at the Academy of Art in Prague, and later made his home at Franzenbad. When the season was over, that is in autumn, winter and spring, he travelled. In 1830–1 he was in Gotha, in 1834–5 in Berlin, in 1839–40 in Vienna. His was altogether an active and, on the whole, prosperous career. He left a diary with notes on human physiognomy, part of which still survives and of which there is a copy in the National Technical Museum in Prague.

During all these years there was a vogue for many kinds of engraved glasses apart from miniatures, all of them what would now be described as souvenirs; but as time passed and mass-production methods took over, they became less and less personal and more and more sentimental and banal. Of the personal gift glasses a four-inch beaker by the rare J.J. Mildner of Gutenbrunn in Lower Austria is an early, sober and distinguished piece. This is dated 1800 and is decorated with the recipient's initials on a red ground, framed by a gilt floral garland. The medallions on his glasses are decorated on the inner side in gold-leaf and red lacquer and are skilfully let in flush with the surface in spaces exactly cut out to receive them; occasionally he would insert in his medallions miniature portraits painted in colours on parchment, and also medallions in the bottoms of tumblers.

Ruins and neo-classical subjects were as popular everywhere during the first thirty or forty years of the nineteenth century as they had been during the final twenty-five years of the eighteenth, and the glass painters followed suit, no doubt influenced a great deal by Wedgwood's jasper ware which had attained so great a success. The most accomplished among the many who catered for this particular taste were the two Mohns: the father, Samuel (1762–1815), who lived in Dresden from 1809 and began his career painting silhouettes on porcelain cups and saucers; the son Gottlob Samuel (1789–1825), who moved to Vienna in 1811 and was patronized by the emperor. A characteristic tumbler by him, its date about 1812, is seen in figure 130, '*La Reconnoisance*', in which a young woman in romantic classical dress with one breast bare stands before an altar holding a basket of fruit. It is a typical, charmingly fanciful sentimental confection which found innumerable imitators. The two Mohns did however break new ground technically by using transparent enamel colours in place of the heavy opaque colours that were in favour with German glass-men in the sixteenth and seventeenth centuries.

This innovation was carried further by the Viennese Anton Kothgasser (1769–1851). Like many other glass-men all over Europe he had had experience as a painter of ceramics, in his case at the Imperial Porcelain Factory in Vienna, had collaborated with the younger Mohn in working in stained glass, and had used on vases and beakers the yellow derived from a compound of silver which had long been common practice in window-glass painting. Three glasses by him are in the Victoria and Albert Museum collection. One of them, presumably from fairly early in the century, is painted with a romantic mountain landscape, black and grey on a clear green ground; it is signed by him and inscribed '*Brühlweg durch das Klausenthal*'. The other two are attributed to the 1830s, by which time he had evidently fallen a victim to the prevailing passion for lavish gilding. Each has a heavy cut foot, one of them painted with a view of St Stephen's in Vienna, the ground gilt all over; the other, no less luscious, has a border of birds, plants, an urn and an obelisk in translucent brown against a black opaque ground.

As with so many other laborious whimsies of the mid-nineteenth century – from Austria, Germany, France, England and elsewhere – I rejoice with smug satisfaction that I am not compelled to live with them. Yet among these weighty *Biedermeier* offerings it is possible to find much good humour and a sense of form in addition, in objects such as the glass signed 'C v S' (for C von Scheidt), its thistle-shaped body with flared neck cut into eight panels, each decorated in coloured enamels with a Chinese juggler. The heavy base is cut with a band of ovals flashed in amber. Von Scheidt was a pupil of Mohn, his earliest work being dated 1816. Figure 131 is a cigar holder and is almost certainly by von Scheidt, though it is not signed; it shows a similar liking for transparent enamels and chinoiserie figures.

But if shapes were clumsy, colours were varied and frequently subtle. The reaction against the taste for a clear crystal upon which the engraver could exercise his precise and delicate skill was almost complete; the market began to demand not only ruby-red and the long familiar green, blue and amethyst, but all kinds of new combinations – a greenish-yellow for instance, a topaz, an amber, used sometimes with opaque-white by means of flashings, thin surface layers which could be cut away to reveal the underlying glass. There were several glass-houses in southern Bohemia, owned by Georg Longueval, Count von Buquoy, that made a speciality of a sealing-wax red and, after 1820, achieved a black opaque glass; to both of these he gave the name 'hyalith'.

The passion – one might almost say the obsession – for colour in great variety was most marked, especially in Central Europe, perhaps a little less enthusiastically elsewhere, and some remarkable *tours de force*, in somewhat doubtful taste, were the result. It was a natural reaction from the earlier liking for clear crystal, whether engraved or no, and it must be confessed that these novelties were as often as not astonishing technical achievements. The black glass, inspired partly it would seem by the popularity of the lugubrious basalt pots and figures devised by Josiah Wedgwood a generation earlier met with immediate, if temporary success.

Another greatly admired type was 'bithyalin', the invention of Friedrich Egermann (1777–1864) of Blottendorf near Haida in Bohemia, who produced it in quantity from 1828 onwards. The medieval glass-maker had always delighted in imitating precious stones, and now modern chemistry allowed experimenters to go much further – to this almost opaque glass marbled in various strong colours (figure 132). It was one of many permutations and combinations. Ruby-red, derived from gold or copper, had been familiar for many years – so were greens, blues and tones of amethyst. Glass-makers now had at their disposal shades of greenish-yellow and yellowish-green derived from uranium, and topaz and amber from a mixture of this and antimony, and with all these colours plus opaque white some elaborate tricks were played with 'flashings'.

Perhaps the decidedly graceless but none the less highly competent skill lavished upon presentation pieces during the first half of the nineteenth century is shown to perfection in the goblet of figure 133, a piece which was seen at Sotheby's in the summer of 1969; it embodies both the worst and the best of the taste of its day, with its heavy, clumsy form, in hyalith glass, its gilding of elaborate scrolling foliage, and its inset medallion of the figure of Justice, seated holding sword and scales, in the *Zwischengold* technique.

Honey, in his handbook to the Victoria and Albert Museum collection, summed up the fashion of the early part of the century in these words:

The forms of the *Biedermeierzeit*, though ultimately derived from classical models, show a characteristic heaviness and lack of classical proportion, with massive feet, bold polygonal facetting and projecting bands of often clumsy cut embossments. The commoner decoration reveals the same coarse vitality, but the more costly pieces, for which there was no small market, often show an exquisite talent, especially in pictorial engraving. The work of many able artists can be identified. Some of these worked independently, to the order of clients at fashionable watering-places such as Teplitz and Karlsbad.

He mentions, of course, Dominik Bimann (1800–57) and August Böhm (1812–90) – the latter was a wanderer, visiting both England and America – and other engravers such as the Pelikan family of Meisterdorf near Kamnitz and the Simms of Jablonec. The chief centres were Bor (Haida) and Steinschonau in Bohemia and Schreiberhau in Silesia; there were the Moser family at Karlsbad, the Pohls at Neuwelt, the Poschingers near Zwiesel in the Bayerischer Wald, the Riedel family at Wilhelmshohe and Polaun in the Isergebirge – all competent and important glass-men, none of them outstanding nor destined to be originators of anything particularly significant.

That honour was reserved for the firm of J. & L.Lobmeyr, and particularly to Ludwig Lobmeyr. The business was started in 1823 and is still directed by members of the family descended from one of the sisters of Josef and Ludwig, the two sons of the founder.

By the middle of the century the glass industry in Central Europe seemed to be set in its ways, commercially enterprising, artistically hidebound, committed more to a museum-inspired copying of the past than to the production of anything startlingly original, unless one can include the wide range of colours already mentioned and the development of overlay glass which, in the fifties, was an important factor in enabling the Bohemian industry to recapture its sadly sagging foreign markets. At that time no one outside Bohemia could imitate this novel overlay glass, which consisted of encasing a core of crystal glass in one or more layers of transparent or opaque coloured glass. The several layers were then cut, disclosing the lower ones according to a previously designed pattern; the results to most modern eyes are interesting rather than particularly agreeable. A specially popular line was opaque-white overlay on a ruby or pink base, its upper layer cut away in patterns and the remaining surface painted and fired with floral designs. Meanwhile the traditional engraving skills had by no means disappeared, although the fashion for colour was at its height. With the hindsight of a century and more later, it is not difficult to see that the whole glass industry of Bohemia (and indeed of other centres) was headed for confusion and frustration; this is not, I hasten to add, true of its down-to-earth commercial mass-production of tableware, whether blown, cut or pressed, which, on the whole, kept to a modest standard of clean, sensible functionalism – (the latter word had not yet been coined) – but of its more ambitious products.

One man – and the Czechs of today give him full credit – who had the vision to lead and the energy, persuasive power and resources to bring some sort of order into comparative chaos, was Ludwig Lobmeyr (1829–1917) of Vienna, who was able to secure the services of the best engravers and designers – professors of the Viennese Academy and the School of Applied Art and men of the calibre of Franz Ulmann (1846–1921), who had been trained at Kamenicky Senov together with several others. By about the 1870s the wind of change was blowing strongly in many dusty corners of the Austrian Empire, especially throughout its traditional glass industry, and the man chiefly responsible for initiating, inspiring and guiding those health-giving breezes was Ludwig.

The Empire's collapse as a result of the First World War, the emergence of Czechoslovakia as a national entity in 1918, the disaster of Hitler's take-over in 1938 and the heart-breaking story of the past quarter of a century have all combined to bedevil any attempt to present a balanced view of the history of the modern industry in what was once Bohemia, or at any rate one that does not offend national susceptibilities. Even language can lead one into error, for the Czech word for Bohemia is 'Czechy', so that one is tempted to label the Bohemian glass industry as Czech, whereas it was mainly owned and directed by Austrians, among them several members of the Lobmeyr family. There was no specifically Czech glass until after 1918, and even afterwards much of the glass produced in the new state should be more accurately described as Austrian. The Lobmeyr firm, for instance, manufactured glass in Czechoslovakia until 1951, and since then has been doing so in modern Austria. One can perhaps sum up the situation by asserting that the Austrian contribution to the development of Bohemian glass was so important that without it neither the Swedish nor the Czechoslovakian industry would have achieved the success they have in the world of today.

The forward-looking Ludwig Lobmeyr was clearly far in advance of his time. I can think of no better evidence than that of the table service of figure 134, which he designed in 1856; it is as clean and simple a set of the highest-quality glass as can be imagined and is well able to stand unashamedly beside the slightly more elongated shapes of the set in figure 135, made by the same firm and designed by Joseph Hoffman in 1920. As examples of the better sort of table-glass, made for use and not merely for ornament, it is no doubt possible to find their equal in many places, but hardly their superior.

But throughout the nineteenth and twentieth centuries the early liking for embellishments, whether in enamelling or in engraving, in addition to the use of colour, remained as much in favour as ever. A superlative example of the use of enamels is seen in figure 136, which shows a beaker designed by Lotte Fink in 1925. Another instance of the way in which the Lobmeyr firm was able to command the services of well-known Viennese painters is the tall vase of figure 137, with its theme of 'architecture'; it is a finely balanced design by Anton Lehmden, carried out by means of wheel-engraving.

A more recent work, one of several specially commissioned presentation pieces, is the covered urn, the '*Schahpokal*' designed and executed for the Federal President of Austria in 1966 for presentation to the Shah of Persia in 1967 on the occasion of his coronation. The coat of arms of the Shah is engraved on one side, that of Austria on the other (figure 138).

There remain two photographs to convey some further notion of the range of Bohemian achievements in modern times. Figure 139 is yet another reminder of the influence of Ludwig Lobmeyr. It is a fine crystal plate 223 millimetres in diameter, its design harking back to the Renaissance; it depicts a boy astride a lioness, a border with floral ornament and the heads of three satyrs, intaglio-cut by Franz Frische for Lobmeyr – a little dry and formal and backward-looking perhaps, but a fine thing none the less, and certainly in advance of its time, somewhere between 1870 and 1885. It shows us the classical tradition about to break out into more fluid manner.

With the admirable *jardinière* of figure 140 we are well into the twentieth century. The form dates from 1945, the engraved wild flowers, so carefully placed on the massive crystal walls of the vessel, could be of any age, culled from nature itself. It was designed in 1935 by Ludvika Smrčková but was not engraved until 1945 by Adolf Matura; when last recorded it was still the property of the designer.

France

While all these varied and often exciting developments were taking place in the Austro-Hungarian Empire, something scarcely less remarkable was happening in France. It has already been noted elsewhere in this book, and not without surprise, that the French, the great masters of the art of the stained-glass window during the twelfth and thirteenth centuries, rarely if ever succeeded in producing any but the most ordinary table and ornamental glass during the seventeenth and eighteenth centuries, when all Europe looked to Paris as the arbiter of fashion and the source of all the embellishments which made for civilized living. But with the nineteenth century, and particularly after about 1840, the French began to establish themselves as glass-men in the modern sense of that honourable word.

The quality of the glass produced in the early years of the century is frankly disappointing, charming though the design can be, as witness the sorbet jug and dish of figure 141, which once graced the table at Malmaison; it is one of a set which belonged to the Empress Josephine, for it is inscribed with the letter 'J' beneath the imperial crown. This is a minor enchantment, but the material of which it is made is quite ordinary.

Fifty years later the glass-works at Clichy-La-Garenne could produce something as fine as the *tazza* of figure 142, which has the bowl, foot and bulb of the stem wheel-engraved with arabesque patterns, intermingled with filaments which terminate in clear spots. It was seen in London at the International Exhibition of 1862, exhibited by M. Maës, one of the founders of the works at Clichy in about 1840. It was one item in the splendid bequest of Felix Slade to the British Museum in 1868, and it was evidently found necessary to apologize for its inclusion in Nesbitt's catalogue of the collection: 'It was selected as one of the best examples of engraving on glass in the

Exhibition, and this must be the excuse for introducing so modern a specimen into this catalogue.' It is pleasant to be able to report that museum officials of today are not ashamed to recognize a fine thing, whatever its date.

The abolition at the Revolution of the ancient privileges so long granted to glass-workers in France forced the industry to stand on its own feet; the march of invention and the progress of chemistry, in France as elsewhere, played havoc with ancient customs. Even so progress came slowly, and the many old-established glass-works in the forests continued to use wood for their furnaces; in 1819 the Saint-Gobain glass-house was still purchasing woodlands to ensure future supplies and was not fully equipped to use coal until 1852. It was a sad period of strikes and unrest, for the workpeople, successors of the 'gentlemen glass-workers' of the past, were as firmly enamoured of special privileges as were their predecessors and made repeated efforts to limit the number of apprentices and to reserve the right of a father to hand on his position to his son. The story is one of fierce competition, of amalgamations, of disputes throughout the whole of the nineteenth century, and is far beyond the scope of this book. We can summarize by saying that the vast expansion of the market resulted at long last in an industrial capacity for the manufacture of utilitarian glass amply sufficient for the country's needs.

This book, though, is concerned with what we clumsily call 'art-glass' and which the French, with more finesse, label '*vases de délectation*'. With the ordinary glass for table or laboratory the French did as well as and no better than their neighbours across the border in Belgium, further east in Germany and Bohemia or across the channel in England; with '*vases de délectation*', thanks to a few highly gifted individuals they astonished the world. The foundation for the remarkable subtleties of the later years of the century was, no doubt, the technical innovations laboriously evolved fifty and seventy years previously – experiments with colour, for example, resulting in the semi-opaque coloured glass called *opaline*, which was all the rage during the middle years of the century.

During the 1830s the pioneer colour glass of Bohemia was being imitated to perfection, and so was that of Venice, which itself had begun to look back to its immensely prosperous past and to revive some of its early specialities. Thus the French were soon making *millefiori* (sections of multicoloured rods embedded in clear glass and cut crosswise), *latticino* (opaque-white threads in fine patterns worked into clear glass) and *aventurine* (spangles of metallic particles melted into clear glass) as to the manner born. The leader in all this was George Bontemps (1799–1884) at the factory of Choisy-Le-Roi near Paris. His success was soon followed by others, notably by Clichy, Baccarat and Saint-Louis.

Baccarat today is probably best known for its admirable clear crystal vases; all three are remembered specially for their mid-nineteenth century production of paperweights, which have been the subject of an enthusiastic cult on both sides of the Atlantic since the Second World War. They were produced by the thousand, filled the novelty shops for years at five shillings and ten shillings each, and now the rarer specimens, like the rarer stamps, fetch thousands on the international market. Bontemps himself is on record in 1851 as saying that 'a single article, paperweights in *millefiori*, has been sold in hundreds of thousands'. The older ones seem to have been made at Saint-Louis and Clichy. Baccarat pieces are sometimes signed with a 'B' and date from 1846 and 1849. Some from Saint-Louis, dating from 1845, are signed 'S.L.'; some from Clichy are signed 'C' and have a characteristic rose, generally pink or white. Those specially in favour depict butterflies, serpents, lizards and flowers of various kinds. Variety of colour and design is infinite. Four typical examples are illustrated in figures 143 and 144, the first a rare flower weight from Baccarat, an apparently unrecorded design. All four weights are from a 1969 sale at Sotheby's.

The Baccarat flower weight in figure 143 has an inner row of six yellow petals of clematis type and an outer row of six white petals striped in pale mauve, a star-dust centre, a single yellow bud, bright green leaves and stalk, set in clear glass above a star-cut base. The three in figure 144 are, from left to right: a Saint-Louis weight, the ground lime-yellow and sunk into it, six alternating loops of blue and pink canes centred on a small cluster of florettes; the one in the centre is also from the Saint-Louis glass-house and depicts a green snake with red eyes and nostrils, the sides with geometric facets, the top cut with a large circular window; the third is a double overlay weight from Clichy, the overlay turquoise on opaque-white cut with six circular windows revealing a concentric *millefiori* mushroom of five rows of canes, including mauve roses. Such ingenious and technically difficult objects were very much to the taste of their day and are now the subject of much earnest study, with prices for rare weights of this character far beyond the average pocket. Indeed they fetch far more than is normally paid for early glass of far greater distinction. The auction prices for these four weights were as follows: figure 143, £3,800; figure 144, from left to right, £800, £1,500 and £1,750.

Another minor development which remained popular for about half a century involved enclosing in crystal glass white cameos and medallions, which acquired a silvery tone in the process and which the French called '*sulfures*' or '*sulphides*'. James Tassie in England had made miniature portraits in an opaque-white glass paste during the 1760s and 1770s. In the last years of the century Desprez in Paris was doing similar work, but during the early days of the Napoleonic Empire he was enclosing them in glass, a process which, in England, was often, but mistakenly, credited to Apsley Pellat. Many of these Desprez miniatures were at first set into glass plaques and framed, but they soon began to be inserted into the sides of such things as scent-bottles and beakers, and later into paperweights. Pellat took out a patent in 1819 and called his process, clumsily, 'crystallo-ceramic' or 'cameo incrustation'. Similar incrustations were also made in Bohemia. Favourite subjects in France were portraits of the various sovereigns and members of their families from Napoleon I to Napoleon III; prominent non-royal and sometimes forgotten personalities of the day; allegories of Liberty and so forth. They were produced in many glass-houses but went out of fashion with the Third Empire.

A much later experiment resulted in *pâte-de-verre*, its originator being the painter and sculptor Henry Cros (1840–1907), an enthusiastic researcher who, after many failures, succeeded in producing a basically glass material (half-way to earthenware), which could be moulded and coloured, a semi-opaque substance which aroused great interest at the time (the 1880s). He had several followers who improved upon his methods without making any very extraordinary contribution to the world's store of beautiful things, for fine glass is such a magnificent metal in itself that it is possible, without necessarily being accused of wilful blindness, to argue that to add an adhesive material is adulteration rather than improvement. A younger contemporary was Albert Dammouse (1848–1926), also a Sèvres technician, whose vases in blue, grey, buff and mauve in an enamel paste resembling soft porcelain were greatly admired when they were shown in the 1900 Paris Exhibition.

Perhaps the best among all the highly accomplished men who experimented with one form or another of *pâte-de-verre* was François Emile Décorchement (b. 1888); he was a sculptor and painter as well as a ceramist and his vases, when he showed them at the 1925 Paris Exhibition, were praised for 'their style, their form and their sober magnificence' – which is a great deal more than can be said for several lesser practitioners. What is one to make of Ringel d'Illzach, whose ashtrays were a great success? They were formed as grimacing masks and one stubbed out one's cigarette in the mouth or eye socket. Perhaps it is not fair to draw attention to him. Almeric Walter, who collaborated with several sculptors during the early years of the twentieth century, is a more rewarding study; he produced vases, ashtrays and paperweights with insects and flowers in green, turquoise, ochre and yellow and ambitious little statuettes of Loie Fuller, the American dancer whose act entranced all Paris, as she danced in many-coloured muslin draperies against a background of electric lights in constantly changing colours.

A further refinement was a substance known as *pâte-de-cristal*, used by Gabriel Argy-Rousseau. It is nearly transparent and gives a clear ring when sounded; it has been used for vases decorated with poppies, anemones and berries in shot-blue, cherry-red and buff, and for lamps modelled by A.Bourraine in the form of jazz-age young women. Whether there is a future for *pâte-de-verre* or for some variation of this powdered glass treatment is anyone's guess. Meanwhile the work of the men chiefly concerned with its development is a subject of considerable interest to collectors today, not so much because of its specialized material, but because its emergence happened to coincide with the movement loosely defined as Art Nouveau, which is now, in the 1970s, very much in fashion.

But it is time to return to the main stream, to two men of the nineteenth century and one of the twentieth who are now recognized as having played a decisive part in the development of the finer kinds of glass. Of these three, two – Eugène Rousseau (1827–91) and Maurice Marinot (1882–1960) – though important, are minor personalities as compared with the third, Emile Gallé (1846–1904), who, whether as theorist, designer, practical glass-man or successful man of business, is the dominating figure of the last twenty years of the nineteenth century.

Eugène Rousseau began his career as a designer of decorative pottery, and was apparently also a dealer in it, but at the age of forty he became fascinated by the possibilities of glass. He designed for the firm of Appert Frères at Clichy and – as was almost inevitable at that time – was much influenced by Japanese art, which was now flooding into Paris. His output was very small and was known only to a small circle of museum experts and amateurs. Three glasses in the Musée des Arts Décoratifs are at once notable and characteristic. The first of these is a champagne-coloured vase, clearly inspired by Japanese pottery, decorated with a landscape in colours. The second – a formidable technical achievement and perhaps the best known of all Rousseau's work – is the so-called Bamboo Vase (the museum bought it in 1878). The main part is square with rounded corners and decorated with a cut and polished design of bamboo leaves, while the swollen centre portion is covered by floral decoration in blue, white and gold. The third is a majestic high-shouldered vase of square sections in which are embedded flame-like streaks of red amid a crackled surface. Another fine piece, designed by Rousseau in 1885 and executed five years later by his pupil and assistant E.Léveillé, is in the Victoria and Albert Museum; it is a covered beaker engraved in a peacock-feather pattern, the glass being champagne-coloured. Rousseau retired and it was Léveillé who was responsible for many handsome pieces after his death – good things but lacking the majestic, monumental quality of the master's personal work.

As often in dealing with modern glass artists, Mrs Ada Polak must be allowed to sum up: 'Nobody since the Venetians of the 16th century had played so cleverly with colour in glass, and as the effects were used in a massive material instead of the brittle Venetian *cristallo*, completely new aesthetic effects were achieved ... The generous size of his vessels, their simplicity of outline, boldness of colour and rich succulence of material all contribute to make his art a truly monumental one.'

Providence endowed Emile Gallé with a wonderfully sensitive eye and a solid, well-established family business at Nancy to fall back on if his early experiments had failed. The firm, owned by his father Charles Gallé, made faience and furniture of the better sort; his mother inherited a mirror factory, and to this Charles added table-glass. Emile acquired the elements of glass manufacture at Meissenthal on the borders of France and Germany and more academic instruction at Weimar; he absorbed also what was to be seen in the museums of Paris and London. At the age of nineteen he was designing glass tableware and helping his father with the pottery side of the business. Two years later he was in command of his own workshop. His great and deserved reputation dates from 1878, when his enamelled glass with gold leaf inserted between the layers and his opaque, coloured and marbled glass made a great impression at the Paris Exhibition. He acquired further fame at the Exhibition of 1884 with all kinds of variations in enamelling, cutting and engraving, based upon ornaments found on such diverse objects as Chinese porcelain, medieval religious art, heraldry and eighteenth-century Bohemian glass.

An already great reputation was enhanced five years later when he showed again at the Paris Exhibition – a moment which has been described as his finest hour, for it was then that the style which is essentially Gallé and unmistakable came to its full flowering. This style springs naturally enough from Gallé's poetic and passionate delight in all the details of flowers and trees and gardens, a delight he shared with the Japanese artists whose work he so much admired. He was no workshop-bound designer laboriously copying from pattern-books, but an enthusiastic gardener and botanist, knowing every vein of every leaf of every tree and as much in love with the ordinary flora of Europe as with more exotic plants from the East: he was as happy with a thistle as with a chrysanthemum. His writings, which are considerable, make this clear enough and go far to explain his success; they also explain what is to most of us in the 1970s his odd habit of often inscribing on a glass a quotation from a poet, the verse inspiring the glass, the glass expressing the thought of the verse; for art, in the view of himself and his friends, should not describe but evoke. What is more it should sweeten life, it should '*adoucir les hommes*'.

All this moral earnestness, this eloquence, this incomparable techni-cal skill would perhaps have been wasted at any other moment in history. As it was the time was exactly right for a Gallé; the cultivated public, bored by the average commercial product of the day, saw in him a deliverer, an apostle of light. What is more – and it does not happen to every idealist – he was immensely successful, so much so that Nancy for a few brief years, instead of being just a busy provin-cial centre, nearly became a place of pilgrimage for the enlightened, while the indirect influence of his style was enormous. If any one man can be said to have invented Art Nouveau it was Gallé.

Success brought its problems. Pupils came, the works expanded; by 1889 there is a large decorators' studio; wooden moulds are made there for the use of the glass-blowers, designs are painted in water-colour, and in the works garden and in the natural history collection are endless models. All this depends upon the ultimate direction of one man, who cannot do everything himself but must inspire and delegate. He writes beautifully: '*Mon œuvre personelle consiste à rêver pour le cristal des rôles tendres et terribles . . . j'impose par avance, autant que je puis, à la matière ondoyante et diverse, les qualités qu'il me convient qu'elle ait, elle et ses colorations, ses arrangements, pour incarner mon rêve, mon dessin*' ('My personal work consists of dreaming up tender and terrible dramatic roles for crystal. As far as I can, I impose in advance on this flowing and varied material the qualities which I consider it possesses – its colours, its form – to bring to life my dream, my design'). Throughout the nineties he soldiers on as enthusiastic as ever and, in the pieces he deals with personally, no less lovingly. A famous example is the 'Dragonfly' in the Conservatoire National des Arts et Métiers in Paris, a cup of blue-grey-mauve against which the body of the insect stands out in contrasting colours and high relief, with part of its body three-dimensional. At the same time less complicated vases in the cased-glass technique were made, many of them in large numbers and of the quality of the 'Oak Vase' in the Victoria and Albert Museum (figure 145), which is decorated with a fluid design of leaves and acorns in shades of green, yellow and brown. It is as notable for the simplicity of its form as for the subtlety of its colours. A thing of this quality would almost certainly be from his own hand; other cased-glass vessels, made with a relief in a single colour (mauve was a favourite) against an opaque-white ground often tinted in waves of colours – (they are often referred to as 'standard Gallé') – would most probably have been made by his staff which, by the year 1900, had increased to three hundred. His final popular triumph was the Paris Exhibition in that year. An example of his table-glass is illustrated in figure 146.

It is inevitable – fallible human nature being what it is – that as soon as any successful practitioner of the arts leaves the scene of his triumphs, many of those who were convinced of his excellence during his lifetime begin to have second thoughts. A few will even dare to register some guarded criticisms before the end. So it was with Emile Gallé. His stand at the Paris Exhibition of 1900 was sensational, filled with technical marvels, but one or two quiet voices, more sorrowful than angry, were heard to whisper regrets for the personal delicacy of the earlier years before he had grown to such proportions. At this distance of time we can perhaps more readily distinguish between what was lasting in his contribution to the art of glass and what was ephemeral.

First of course was his technical expertise – cutting, engraving, enamelling, colours and the rest; that in itself would be sufficient to establish him as the greatest glass-man of his generation, as the Frenchman who was most influential in raising the standard of his country's glass industry as a whole, and in forcing a wide public to realize that there can be more to this ravishing material than its practical use in home and laboratory, immensely important though that is. Less easy to assess is the influence of his style. I hold the decidedly heretical view that, in spite of numerous imitators, it died with him in 1904 because it was so personal. But the theories behind it did not die: the love of nature in all its aspects (I could well have written 'worship' instead of 'love') as the foundation of all excellence, the faith that it was the mission of art – all art – to sweeten life. This missionary faith would surely have been his had he been brought up in other circumstances and guided towards other means of expression. As it is the world has reason to be grateful that Gallé was born at the appropriate time, in the appropriate place and to the family most suited to foster his exceptional talents.

He is honoured in many quarters as the chief architect of that indefinable style known as Art Nouveau, and it is true enough that there is something in the fluid quality of glass that lends itself to the curves of a style which so readily transforms itself into a tedious mannerism. But Art Nouveau would have entranced the fashionable world of the 1890s and 1900s if Gallé had never existed. It derived from many sources, certainly not from Gallé alone, and the fact that he designed and made so many pieces which, after three-quarters of a century, we inevitably associate with it, merely shows that, originator though he was, he was sensitive to the climate of opinion of his day, not its sole begetter.

There is now (1971) renewed interest in all the many aspects of Art Nouveau and a correspondingly eager search for even the most ordinary examples from his factory and, to a lesser degree, for the products of his many followers, the nearest of them, both geographically and in spirit, being the glasses made by his neighbours in Nancy, the firm of Daum, founded in 1875. The founder's two sons, Auguste and Antonin, learned much from Gallé and began to make flower-decorated glasses in his manner in 1890 (figure 147). Similar 'standard Gallé' types of glass were made nearby at Lunéville and also at Sèvres and over the border in Belgium at Val-Saint-Lambert. His influence was also felt in Sweden and Norway, and also in the United States, where L. C. Tiffany (1848–1933), a no less gifted personality, became as important an international figure as Gallé himself.

All this was changed by the First World War. Art Nouveau and its charming, rounded, liquid forms and rather self-conscious artistry were now out of date – and so was the fashion for elaborate ornamentation. Instead the applied arts more or less followed the example of the mistress art, architecture: form must not be imposed from outside but be determined by the nature of the material, growing naturally from it; surfaces should be uncluttered; shapes should be derived from function. There was nothing particularly new about the theory, for something of the sort was probably in the minds of the builders of the Temple of Karnak, of the Parthenon, and of Stonehenge, but its application during the years between the two wars was changing the face of Europe. Glass-men, perhaps without any very conscious volition, inevitably followed suit and everywhere, particularly in France, the mood was, on the whole, one of cool astringency. Among several personalities of exceptional talent during these years two are outstanding, one of them a dedicated artist whose output was extremely small but his influence was great, the other a prolific, ingenious manufacturer who exactly caught the spirit of the times with a great variety of clear, highly stylized patterns.

The first of these two gifted men is Maurice Marinot (1882–1960), one of the original Fauves – Matisse and Derain among them – who with their bold use of primary colours made so startling an impact upon the art scene in the years from about 1904 to 1914. But Marinot, entranced by the possibilities of glass, deserted painting and spent twenty-seven years, from 1922 until his health gave way, in exploring and mastering its technicalities. 'Each time,' he said, 'it is a marvellous fight [*une belle bataille*], a profound pleasure in the physical effort.' At first he decorated his work with enamels, then experimented with acid-etching (Gallé had also used this method) and, after about 1922, blew every piece personally. His vases and bottles are simple, solid, monumental shapes, some composed of inlays of colours between layers of thick transparent glass, others of a foam of air-bubbles amid a glass tinted a greyish-yellow and next to impossible to illustrate adequately except in colour. His output was necessarily extremely limited and his pieces are very rarely seen on the market. (A small bottle turned up in a Sotheby sale in the autumn of 1970 and made £600.)

The second glass technician to achieve a highly personal style was René Lalique (1860–1945), who was well known by the beginning of the century as a designer of Art Nouveau jewellery, in which glass pastes were freely used. He was greatly encouraged to enlarge his repertoire by a commission from Coty for a series of perfume bottles. In 1908 he started a modest glass-house, making mostly blown glass, but his real success began in 1918 when he moved to a larger factory at Wingen-sur-Moder. He can be said to have imposed upon the world of fashion between the wars, and particularly during the 1920s, the ice-cool formal patterns in relief on all kinds of vases, bowls and jars, mostly of colourless glass with a frosted surface, which are characteristic of his style. Colour is used but rarely and his glass was hailed as having 'the ethereal brilliance of Arctic ice'. Some of his larger vessels could only be made singly, while the rest of his vast output was produced by the hundred, and his influence was felt throughout all the decorative arts. Few men can be said to have so fully represented the ideals of those two decades.

At least two glass-workers in France must be mentioned as followers of Marinot and of nearly as high a standard: André Thuret (b. 1898), working mostly in slightly tinted transparent glass, and Henri Navarre (b. 1885) a sculptor who turned to glass in the 1920s. The firm of Daum in Nancy was at first influenced almost entirely by Gallé, but in about 1920, looking about for a style more in keeping with postwar ideals, turned to Marinot and produced some simpler but notable vases in his manner.

Sweden

It would be difficult to overestimate the influence exercised upon modern glass manufacture by the example of the Scandinavian countries, and particularly by Sweden. Up to the twentieth century glass in all the northern countries more or less followed the rest of Europe, but from the time of the First World War it developed a style of its own which, though not easy to define, is immediately recognizable. The credit belongs chiefly to the Swedes, partly because of the exceptional talents of two gifted men, Simon Gate and Edward Hald, who were engaged in 1916 and 1917 as designers to the glass-works at Orrefors. But it must also be remembered that Sweden has taken a highly civilized interest in all the applied arts for many years and was a pioneer in discussing such matters seriously.

The Swedish Society of Industrial Design (the *Svenska Slöjd-foreningen*) was founded as long ago as 1845 for the encouragement and guidance of national crafts and, on the whole, avoided the worst excesses of mid-nineteenth-century taste. But the First World War, while bringing great prosperity to every neutral country, brought also many shortages of all kinds of goods, and forced manufacturers to simplify design. Add to this circumstance the already consciously biased public taste in favour of clean lines and lack of fuss in every sort of household goods and the stage was set for the remarkable performance of Swedish industry of every kind during the past half-century.

Theories no doubt gave the designers their opportunity, but the theories would hardly have resulted in practical results had the market not been already conditioned in their favour. The theories briefly were those of what has come to be known as Functionalism, which is merely another word for fitness for purpose. The advertising slogan 'Handsome Household Wares' was coined in 1915 and was soon followed by 'Let the Artist design for Industry'. Within a few years the products of Swedish industry were admired all over Europe, not least its glass. Simon Gate and Edward Hald were both painters. The former (1883–1945), a farmer's son, was trained at the Academy in Stockholm, the latter (b. 1883), a townsman from Stockholm, had been a pupil of Matisse in Paris. Hald had had a little experience in designing pottery, but neither he nor Gate knew anything about glass; each had to start at the beginning.

The oldest glass factory in Sweden is Kosta, founded in 1742. The Orrefors factory – there was an iron-foundry there in the eighteenth century – began in a very modest manner in 1898, but went speedily ahead as soon as Gate and Hald had been engaged. Two types of luxury glass are particularly associated with them. The first is the glass known as 'Graal Glass' (figure 148), a development of the characteristic Gallé manner which the factory had been imitating until their arrival. In a Gallé glass the finish was the concern of the decorators – that is, cutting out the pattern from the varicoloured layers (the casings). In Graal glass this was an intermediate process, the final result having to be fixed in the furnace, by which the ornament would appear to melt into, rather than be cut away from, the background. Each man designed for Graal glass, Gate mostly depicting figures in movement in many colours, Hald working rather in fluid line.

So far the fame of the factory was confined to Sweden itself, both for Graal glass and for engraving. It was the latter as practised by both artists that placed Orrefors firmly and permanently upon the international map. It was this engraved glass that enjoyed so great a success at the Paris Exhibition of 1925, each man contributing his own highly personal style. Gate made use of stories from the Bible and classical mythology, the meeting of Solomon and the Queen of Sheba is a famous later (1938) example; Hald preferred playful subjects and shallow linear engravings.

The year 1930, also at Orrefors, witnessed the development of the glass known as Ariel, described at the factory as 'organized air-bubbles', which has been combined with various coloured inlays and also with the Graal method. A more recent innovation at Orrefors is the so-called 'Ravenna' glass, developed by Sven Palmquist after the Second World War; it is a distinct style of heavy transparent tinted glass inlaid with geometrical patterns. If Orrefors remains the most important of the Swedish glass-houses, Kosta did not lag so very far behind and secured the services of Vicke Lindstrand, who had been trained at Orrefors, as its chief designer in 1950. Two other Orrefors pieces are illustrated in figures 149 and 150.

Thanks to a galaxy of very bright recruits since the early experimental days of Gate and Hald, Orrefors continues to hold its exceptional position; at the same time more than a dozen Swedish glass-works followed its example and employed professional designers with immense benefits to the industry as a whole. Among many gifted individuals, the name of Edvard Stromberg (1872–1946) will always be remembered with particular respect because of the glass he and his wife executed during his last years (from 1933 until his death) in his own small establishment, never making 'coloured' glass as the term is generally understood, but the finest crystal in very subtle tones of grey, mauve or pale blue, and no less subtle line and mass; this tradition was continued by his widow, Gerda, who died in 1960.

The example of Sweden in engaging artists from outside the glass industry as designers for both tableware and so-called 'art glass' – the latter an odious term which shows few signs of going out of circulation – was followed in the other Scandinavian countries, as elsewhere.

Norway

In Norway Sverre Pettersen (1884–1959) joined the factory at Hadeland in 1928, adding tableware and engraved glass to his interests in textiles, stained-glass and bookbinding. Glasses engraved with personal designs for individual purchasers were agreeable and popular products. After the Second World War two young men, each of them twenty-six years old, were engaged as designers and greatly increased the range of the factory's products. One of them, Willy Johansson, has experimented with various coloured effects, including a ruby-red glass changing to sea-green lower down. The other, Herman Bongard, works also in pottery, silver and wood. A younger man, Arne Jon Jutrem, joined the firm at the age of twenty-one in 1950 and made his name with vases of bubbled green glass and with vessels of transparent glass with coloured spirals.

Denmark

In Denmark the Holmegaard glass-works owe a great debt to the architect Jacob Bang, appointed in 1925 at the age of twenty-six. He left in 1942, and Per Lütken reigned in his stead. More recently – since 1955 – Bang, with the assistance of several young people, has designed glass for the factory of Kastrup, until then occupied almost entirely with providing bottles for breweries.

Finland

In Finland the factory at Riihimäki was advised by Henry Ericsson (1898–1933) and also by Arttu Brummer (1891–1951), Director of the Central School of Arts and Crafts in Helsinki. A later and interesting development was the manufacture of vases at Karhula-Iittala to the designs of the architect Alvar Aalto; they are reminiscent of the simple lines of the bent-wood furniture of which, in the 1930s, he was a pioneer.

But the greatest name in Finnish glass history is that of a woman, Gunnel Nyman, whose death at the age of only forty in 1948 deprived her country of a highly original and sensitive talent, seen to perfection in her many simple but very subtle 'folded' models and – perhaps even more engagingly – in vessels in which areas of shallow cutting provided a contrast to large smooth surfaces in between. Other notable Finnish designers since her death were first Tapio Wirkkala (b. 1915) (figure 151) and Timo Sarpaneva (b. 1926).

Holland

There is only one factory in Holland which produces tableware and decorative glass: the Royal Dutch Glassworks at Leerdam, near Rotterdam, which was founded as long ago as 1765. It came into line with the general fashion for simple, severe, clear-cut shapes about the time of the First World War and at least two designers have played a notable part in its progress. The first of them was Chris Lebeau, a general designer who worked for the factory in 1922 and 1923. When he left his place was taken by Andries Copier.

Modern Venice

The exciting developments in France, in Austria and Czechoslovakia, and later in Scandinavia during the last 150 years are liable, a little unfairly perhaps, to divert attention from what was taking place at more or less the same period in the one place in Europe with a tradition of glass manufacture going back eight hundred years. Venice, with its long-standing near-monopoly, is the heiress of Near-Eastern know-how, and the actual, if generally unwilling school-mistress of all Europe in the craft of the glass technician. Until after the First World War Italian glass-factories produced little more than clever pastiches of the styles of the distant past; they seemed to be eternally looking back over their shoulders. Two exceptional men gave them a new direction and, so to speak, pushed them into the modern world.

The first of these, perhaps the most original, was Paolo Venini, from near Milan, who in 1921, with a Venetian called Giacomo Cappellin, founded a glass-house in Murano. The new firm met with considerable success at the 1925 Paris Exhibition with pieces copied or adapted from early Venetian glasses as seen in old paintings, the glass being transparent, either colourless or tinted pale blue, green or amethyst. After that Venini operated alone, designing a great deal himself, sometimes employing artists from outside, and always in close contact with the lively, forward-looking and by now fashionable group of young designers centred on Milan, notably Gio Ponti, whose ideas on modern decoration in every form can be seen in the back-numbers of the magazine *Domus*.

Venini now began experimenting with various colours and textures, reproducing old tricks (for instance *millefiori*, or as the Romans had it, *murrine* – the word is still used in Murano) and playing with new ones, three in particular: *vetro pulegoso* is opaque and contains numerous small, close air-bubbles; *vetro corroso*, as its name implies, is treated with acids to give it an apparently corroded surface; *vetro sommerso* is bubbly glass, encased in some transparent material. The forms were simple, colour and texture infinitely varied (figure 152). Those who worked for him from time to time included the sculptor Napoleon Martinuzzi, the architect Tommaso Buzzi, and the Swedish potter Tyra Lundgren. For his post-Second World War glass he made further experiments: *vetro tessuto* – threads of contrasting colours embedded in the glass; and *vetro pezzato* – a patchwork of squares in contrasting colours.

The second man of outstanding ability is Ercole Barovier, the descendant of a glass-making family which can be traced to the fifteenth century. By the end of the 1920s he had produced a glass he called *primavera*, with a mottled surface; 1940 witnessed the birth of *vetro rugiada*, with a surface that looked as if it was covered with a fine dew, *vetro gemmato*, with texture like natural stone, and various other permutations. Among these are *vetro barbarico* – opaque with a rough surface; *vetro ramarro* – 'lizard' glass, mottled green; *vetro damasco*, coloured mosaic dusted with gold and *vetro parabolico* – patchwork (figure 153).

Other modern designers and makers who have also contributed to the postwar renaissance of Italian glass are Flavio Poli, chief designer to the firm of Seguso Vetri d'Arte; Archimede Seguso (figure 154); the Arte Vetraria Muranese where Giulio Radi, who died in 1952, made great play with metallic effects on surfaces; and – among others – Gino Genedese, who seems to regard glass as if it were stone almost ready to be sculptured.

Thanks to the enterprise in 1950 of Il Centro Studio Pittori nell'arte del Vetro artists from outside were encouraged to submit designs. A few men of the calibre of Picasso, Chagall and Kokoschka were attracted, but contacts, according to Mrs Ada Polak, have not been lasting. This is hardly surprising, for a glass-man, if he is to accomplish anything out of the ordinary in so delicate a *métier*, must be dedicated to the craft – it is hardly sufficient to have great, even overwhelming talent in a wider field.

Finally, one other glass artist of the twentieth century must be mentioned who, though German-born and for the final twenty-one years of his life professor in cutting and engraving on precious stones at Stuttgart, does not quite fit into a rigid national frame. This is Wilhelm V. Eiff (1890–1943), son of a workman at a branch of the Württembergische Metallwarenfabrik; after learning the rudiments of engraving on metal and glass locally, he wandered around in the spirit of his medieval forbears, working wherever he could find a job to his liking. He was, for instance, for a time in the studio of Lalique, and he was also with the glass-engraver Charles Michel, while in 1921 he did some engraving for Stephan Rath of the firm of

Lobmeyr in Vienna. He was an exceptional person with that great gift that is denied to so many who are in other respects masters of their craft – the ability to pass on to others not merely the technique of their trade but an abiding enthusiasm for every aspect of it. By all accounts, during his years at Stuttgart pupils came to him from all over the world, so that, thirty years after his death, his influence is still felt from Scandinavia to Japan. No teacher could wish for a finer memorial. He was, above all, an engraver, equally at home with a miniature portrait made up from the finest thread-like lines or in high relief. He also, in the thirties, invented an engraving tool which made possible the execution of engraved windows on a monumental scale.

Epilogue

It is next to impossible to form a considered judgement about one's contemporaries. These words are written during the last weeks of 1970. Looking back over the past one can distinguish certain fairly distinctive threads which have all played their part in the pattern of a tapestry which has taken about two thousand years to reach its present state, and it is refreshing to realize that there can be no finality. Each generation is liable, as the ingenuity of a few gifted individuals, most of them anonymous, sets up new standards for the treatment of this most flexible of materials, to imagine that it is adding a final chapter to the long story, and finds it difficult to believe that other eyes and other hands will devise new methods and experiment with fresh juxtapositions of colours and shapes. Who, for instance, in Rembrandt's lifetime, could have foreseen a Watteau or a Turner? We already turn a nostalgic eye towards the subtleties of a glass by Gallé or by Gate, and can see them in perspective; such things will never be made quite like that again. It will be fun for our successors a hundred years hence to look back at us and make up their minds whether or not the last years of the twentieth century were worthwhile in terms of this delectable, magical metal.

Appendix: Rock-Crystal

From the earliest times glass-makers could not fail to notice how closely their material resembled certain precious and semi-precious stones. The ancient Egyptians succeeded in making small glass objects that could, without too close a look, be mistaken for amethyst or lapis lazuli. Venice, by the fifteenth century, had discovered, or rather rediscovered, that the use of manganese had the effect of decolorizing the normal yellowish glass of their day, but it should be noted that such clear glass is rare – their market at that time, and indeed later, preferred colours. But the clear glass thus produced was called *cristallo*, an obvious enough indication that they had in mind its resemblance to rock-crystal, which was greatly admired and carved in medieval Egypt, Iraq and Persia. (There is for instance – one among several such examples – a ewer of carved rock-crystal in the Treasury of St Mark's which bears a dedication to the Fatimid Sultan of Egypt, who ruled from AD 975 to 996.) Modern practice in engraving on glass can be traced back to the rock-crystal carving carried out at the court of the Emperor Rudolf II (1576–1612) at Prague by his court lapidary Caspar Lehmann (1570–1612), and by gifted Italian craftsmen of the calibre of Ottavio Miseroni, who was summoned to Prague from Milan in 1588 and during the next thirty-five years worked for three emperors in succession.

It is not without significance that half a century later, when in England George Ravenscroft was granted his patent for seven years, the document used these words: 'a new sort of crystalline glass resembling rock-crystal'. Obviously, as rock-crystal was rare a substitute which could be engraved and cut attracted attention and rapidly took its place. It was, however, used to some extent, certainly throughout the seventeenth century, for specially luxurious objects, of which the gold and enamel-mounted vase illustrated here is one of several from the Arturo Lopez–Willshaw Collection, which was seen at Sotheby's in 1970 (figure 155).

From this kind of cutting to the commercial cutting of innumerable chandeliers and table services of the eighteenth and early nineteenth centuries is no great step. Figure 156 is an admirable example of a table candelabrum, also of rock-crystal, from the late seventeenth or early eighteenth centuries; it turned up in a sale at Christie's earlier in the same year. Figure 157, from one of Sotheby's mineral sales, is simply a block of rock-crystal as extracted from mother earth.

Selected Bibliography

Masterpieces of Glass, Harden, D.B., Painter, K.S., Pinder-Wilson, R.H., Tait, H.S., The British Museum, 1968

Glass: A Handbook and Guide to the Museum Collection, Honey, W.B., Victoria and Albert Museum, 1946

Bohemian Glass, Uresova, L., Victoria and Albert Museum, 1965

Barrelet, James, *La Verrerie en France*, Larousse, 1953

Barrington Haynes, E., *Glass through the Ages*, Penguin Books, 1948

Buckley, Wilfred, *The Art of Glass*, Phaidon Press, 1939

Davis, Frank, *The Country Life Book of Glass*, 1966

Frothingham, Alice, *Spanish Glass*, Faber and Faber, 1964

Gros-Galliner, Gabriella, *Glass – a guide for collectors*, Frederick Muller, 1970

Hudig, Ferrand, *Dutch Glass Engravers*, privately printed, 1926

Mariacher, Giovanni, *Italian Blown Glass*, Thames and Hudson, 1961

Neuberg, Frederic, *Glass in Antiquity*, translated by R.J.Charleston, Art Trade Press, 1949

Pesatova, Zuzana, *Bohemian Engraved Glass*, Hamlyn, 1968

Polak, Ada, *Modern Glass*, Faber and Faber, 1962

Index

Aalto, Alvar 110
Academy of Art, Prague 88
Achilles 4
Albuquerque, Duke of 27
Alchemists 15
Alexandria 14
Alicante 28
Altare 11–13
'Amiens Chalice' 69
Andalusia 23, 29
Anne of Austria 27
Antioch 14
Antwerp 10, 13–15, 36, 37
Appert Frères 100
Ariel Glass 108
Argy-Rousseau, Gabriel 99
Art-Glass 96
Art Nouveau 100, 102, 104–6
Austro-Hungarian Empire 87, 93, 95
Aventurine Glass 16, 87

Baar, Armand 49
Baccarat 50, 97
Bang, Jacob 109
Barbarini Palace 4
Barcelona 21, 25, 27
Barilla 28
Barovier, Domingo 27, 31
Belgium 3, 96
Berlin 88
Bidermier 90, 91
Biemann or Bimann, Dominik 88, 92
Bithyalin 91

Blottendorf 91
Blowing 5
Bohemia 20, 73–86, 90, 92–4, 98
Bohemian 87, 92, 96
'Bohemian crystal' 77
Bohm, August 92
Bonaparte, Joseph 33
Bongard, Herman 109
Bonhomme 14, 37, 48
Bontemps, George 97
Bordoni (of Altare) 12
Bourraine, A. 99
Brescia 13
Briati 20
Britain 25
British Museum 3, 4, 9, 16, 20, 37, 95
Brittany 58
Brummer, Arthur 110
Brun, Sigismund 32
Burghley Nef 22
Byzantine Empire 10

Cadalso 30, 31
Cadibona mountain pass 11
Cameo incrustation 98
Cappellin, Giacomo 111
Cassel 13
Castile 30–32
Castle Eden, Co. Durham 8
Catalonia 25
Charles VI of France 52
Choisy-Le-Roi 97
Christie's 86

Index

Clear Crystal 90, 91
Clichy-La-Garenne 95, 97, 98
Cluny Museum 68
Cologne 36
Conservatoire National des Arts et
    Métiers, Paris 103
Constantinople 10
Copier, Andries 110
Cordoba 24, 29
Cristallo 101
Cros, Henry 98
Cutting 5
Czechoslovakia 73, 93

Da Costa 13
Dagnia 13
Dammouse, Albert 99
Dark Ages 9
Daum, Antonin 104
Daum, Auguste 104
Daum, firm of 104, 106
Décorchement, François Emile 99
Denmark 109
Desprez 98
Diamond engraved 84
Diamond-point 20, 40-3, 85
Differences in basic formula 1
d'Illzach 99
Dresden 89

Egermann, Friedrich 91
Egypt 3
Eiff, Wilhelm 112
El Escorial 31
Elizabeth 37
England 87, 98
Ericsson, Henry 110
Eugene, Prince 81

Façon d'Angleterre 65-7
Façon de Bohème 65-7

Façon de Venise 10, 14, 20
Fairfax Cup 16
Farnese, Queen Isabella 32
Ferdinand, Archduke 84
Ferdinand, Catholic King of Spain 26
Ferdinand III of Castile 29
Ferdinand VII, King of Spain 34
Ferrara 10
Fink, Lotte 94
Finland 110
Flashings 90, 91
Florence 19
France 50-72, 95-106
Franks Bequest 37
Franzenbad 88
Frederick Augustus, Elector of
    Saxony 85
Frische, Franz 94
Frotheringham, Mrs Alice 26

Gallé, Charles 101
Gallé, Emile 51, 100-5, 108
Garnier 52
Gate, Simon 107, 108
Genoa 15
Germany 96
Gibbon, Edward 24
Glass makers privileges in France
    52-53, 56
Glassworks, Royal Dutch at Leerdam
    110
Goldleaf 89, 101
Gonzaga 13
Gotha 88
Goya 24
Goyeneche 31
Graal Glass 108
Great Exhibition 87
Greenwood 36, 44, 45
Gridolphi 47
Grisaille 84
Gutnebrunn 88

Hald, Edward 107–8
Hall-in-Tyrol 13, 84–5
Hamilton, Sir William 4
Hochschnitt 76, 80, 82
Hochstetter, Sebastian 84
Hoffman, Joseph 94
Holland 110
Holmegaard works 109
Howell, James 2, 28
Honey, W.B. 18, 91
Humpen 86
Hungary, King of (Mathias Corvinus) 17
Hyalith 90, 91

Ice Glass 17
Imperial Porcelain Factory, Vienna 89
Intaglio-cut 94
International Exhibition 95
Isabella, Queen 26
Islamic conventions 25
Italians in France 59
Italy 10

Jasperware 89
Johansson, Willy, 109
Josephine, Empress 96
Juttrem, Arne Jon 109

Kamenicky Senov 93
Kastrup factory 109
Killinger, Georg Friedrich 85
Koc of Dobos 81
Kosta 107–8
Kothgasser, Anton 89
Kunckel 78

La Granja De San Ildefonso 23, 32–4
Lalique, René 106
Lambotte 31
Latticino 17, 18, 22, 97
Lebeau, Chris 110

Lehman, Caspar 75, 76, 85
Leopold I, Emperor 81
Léveillé, E. 100
Liebsteinsky von Kolowrat, Count Franz Karl 84
Liège 13, 14, 39
Lindstrand, Vicke 108
Lobmeyr, Josef and Ludwig 92
Lobmeyr, Louis 74
Lobmeyr, Ludwig 92–4
Loire Valley 57
London Museum 37
Longueval, Georg, Count von Buquoy 90
Lunadi 82
Lunéville 104
Lutken, Per 109
Lycurgus Cup 3–5
Lyons 55

Madrid 23, 32, 33
Maes, M. 25
Mallorca 25, 27
Malmaison 96
Mansell, Sir Robert 2, 13, 28
Mariachers, Giovanni 10
Marinot, Maurice 100, 105–6
Mary of England (Princess Royal) 41, 44
Matura, Adolf 95
Medici porcelain 19
Meissen 19
Meissenthal 101
Meyer, J.F. 86
Millefiori 16, 97–8, 111
Mildner, J.J. 88
Mirrors 20
Modern Venice 110–12
Mohn, Gottlob Samuel 89
Mohn, Samuel 89–90
Monferrato, Signori di 12
Montagu, Lady Mary Wortley 15

Mooleyser, Willem 41
Moser 92
Moulding 5
Murano 2, 9, 10, 14, 18, 27
Musée des Arts Decoratifs 71, 100
Muslims 24
Mustapha II, Sultan 81

Nancy 101, 102, 104, 106
Napoleon I 98
Napoleon II 98
Napoleonic 87, 98
National Technical Museum, Prague
    88
Navagero, Andrea 26
Navarre, Henri 106
Neri, Antonio 15, 78
Nero, Emperor 5
Netherlands 36–49
Nevers 13, 55, 60–62
Newcastle 83
Normandy Monopoly 58
Norway 109
Nový Svět 88
Nuremberg 13, 85
Nyman, Gunnel 110

Oak Vase 103
Opaline 96
Opaque-white glass 19, 84, 90, 92, 98,
    103
Orange, Prince of 40, 41
Orrefors 107–8
Overlay glass 92

Palmquist, Sven 108
Paperweights 97–8
Paris Monopoly 58
Paris Exhibition 1925 99, 108, 111
Parr, Sir William 37
Passglas 85–6
Pâte de Cristal 99

Pâte de verre 98–9
Peleus 4
Pelikan family 92
Pellat, Apsley 98
Perrot, Bernard 62
Petronius 5
Pettersen, Sverre 109
Philip II, King of Spain 27
Pohls, 92
Poitiers 24
Polak, Mrs Ada 101
Polaun 92
Portland Vase 3, 4, 78
Poschingers 92
Potsdam 78–9, 81
Praun, Jacob and Clara 83
Preissler, Ignatz 84
Purple of Cassius 78

Raimondi 17
Raphael 17
Ravenna Glass 108
Ravenscroft, George 1, 69, 83
Réaumour 61–2
Riano, Juan 23
Riedel 92
Rodriguez 29
Roemer 40, 79–80
Roman Glass 3
Rome 3
Rome, Twilight of 8–22
Rousseau, Eugene 100
Rudolph II, Emperor 75

Saint-Gobain 50, 96
Saint-Louis 50, 97
Salome 15
Sang, David 46
Sarpaneva, Timo 110
Savona 11
'Savoy Vase' 70
Saxon 82, 85–6
Schaffgotsch, Count 76, 81–2

Schaper, John 82
School of Applied Art, Vienna 93
Schreiberhau 92
Schurman, Anna Maria von 41
Schwanhardt, Georg 76
Schwartz, S. 81
Schwarzlot 82, 84
Schwinger, Hermann 85
Serpent-stem glasses 39
Sevilla 29–30
Sèvres 99, 104
Sheba, Queen of 15
Silesia 73, 81
Sit, Ventura 32
Slade Bequest, 16, 95
Smith, Walter F. 23, 34, 38
Smrčková, Ludvika 95
Solomon 15
Sotheby's 39, 91, 97, 106
Spain 3, 21, 23–35
Stangenglas 42, 79, 80, 83
Stipple engraving 44
Stockholm 107
Strasbourg Museum 72
Stromberg, Edvard 108
Stromberg, Gerda 109
Sweden 104, 106–9
Swedish Society of Industrial Design
    107
Syria 3, 14

Tassie, James 98
Tazza 95
Thetis 4
Thuret, André 106
Tiffany, L.C. 104

Trailing 8
Turin 11

Ulmann, Franz 93

Val-Saint-Lambert 104
Vases de délectation 96
Venetian tradition 24, 38, 53, 54, 55
Venice 9, 14–17, 20–1, 84
Venini, Paolo 111
Venus 17
Verzelini 14, 27
Victoria and Albert Museum 16, 20,
    22, 32, 83, 85, 89, 100, 103
Vienna 88–90, 93
Vilkums 81
Visigoths 24
Visscher, Anna Roemers 41
Visscher, Maria 41
Von Scheidt, C. 90

Waddesdon Bequest 17
Walpole, Horace 19
Walter, Almeric 99
Wedgwood 89, 91
Weimar 101
Wheel-engraved 95
Whistler, Lawrence 44
William II of Orange 41
William III of England 41
Wingen-sur-Monder 106
Winter, Friedrich 76
Wirkkala, Tapio 110
Wolf, David 45–6

Zwischengoldglas 77, 82, 83, 91

WITHDRAWN
No longer the property of the
Boston Public Library.
Sale of this material benefits the Library.